*"If you ho...   ...nation
on prayer techniques in thi...   ...easy
ans... often do not help in areas such ...   ...which most of us
struggle, either in understanding or practising... ...is is a significant
book that helps readers to think more deeply about prayer and to grow
in their life of prayer. Using his considerable skills and experience as an
accomplished scientist, able theologian, wise pastor and honest disciple
of Christ, David Wilkinson tackles the question of prayer from various
angles with wit and wisdom, unmasking popular myths, bringing out
tensions, and offering assurances based on Scripture. Writing poignantly
from his own personal experience, David Wilkinson addresses the
reality of why God answers our prayers but also why our prayers often
go unanswered. He is an astute guide who leads us to explore scientific
ideas such as quantum physics and chaotic systems to shed some light to
our quest. At the end, he brings us to the God of the Bible who cannot
be put into a pigeonhole but who loves us and relates with us in his
sovereign will as his story unfolds from creation to new creation. We are
challenged to respond by trusting him and expressing that trust through
deepening and authentic prayer."*

**Bishop Robert Solomon, Bishop Emeritus of The Methodist
Church in Singapore**

*"This is an exciting book because it comes from a writer who has
engaged deeply and skilfully with science, the Bible and human
experience, and refuses to short-change any of them. The style is
accessible, intelligent and humane, and the result is a book which will be
profoundly helpful and encouraging to anyone trying to pray with both
heart and mind."*

Bishop John Pritchard, former Bishop of Oxford

"Imagine sitting down with a physicist and a theologian over coffee with the topic of prayer decided on in advance as the subject of the conversation. That's exactly what you get in David Wilkinson's fascinating new book on prayer, as he is both that scientist and that theologian and is having this conversation with himself and allowing us to listen in. I know of no other book on prayer even remotely like this one. It is at the same time fascinating, challenging, inspiring, humbling, humorous, profound, you can derive from it a lot of different things. Like what has been said about the Gospel of John you can plug into this conversation at whatever level that suits you. On the one hand the discussion is shallow enough for a baby to wade in. On the other it is deep enough for an elephant to drown! I highly recommend this book on prayer – it may change not merely your prayer life, but the whole way you look at life!"

Ben Witherington, III, Amos Professor of New Testament for Doctoral Studies, Asbury Theological Seminary

"In this book, David wrestles with the themes of prayer, science and the nature of God with his characteristic humility, vulnerability, wisdom, and passion to remain dissatisfied with easy answers. This is the book I wish I'd read years ago, and to which I will return time and again into the future. If you have ever struggled with whether (and why) God answers some prayers and not others, this book is for you."

Rev'd Dr Joanne Cox-Darling, Regional coordinator, London: Discipleship and Ministries Learning Network, The Methodist Church

"If you are terrified by books on prayer this isn't one of those books! This combines humour, personal experience and informed intelligence. Rather than amplify human effort in praying, David walks us through *all the obstacles to prayer into a new awareness of the God who responds to people trying to find him. An excellent read."*

– **Joel Edwards, International Director, Micah Challenge and former General Director, Evangelical Alliance UK**

"In our complex and often confusing world, the tendency is to look for easy answers, avoiding the tough and perplexing questions that confront us. We simplify, formularize, regularize and codify; an exercise in reductionism which at times can be a mask for arrogance, self-deception or downright laziness. No area is this more evident than in the subject of prayer.

"In this highly readable and positively provocative book, When I Pray, What Does God Do?, *renowned scholar, astrophysicist, theologian and pastor, Professor David Wilkinson, a man who is eminently qualified to do so, addresses this age-old and still thorny question; namely, the problem of how God responds to prayer. Professor Wilkinson tackles the subject with the rigour of a scientist, the spirit of a theologian, the heart of a shepherd and the humility of a disciple who is on a personal pilgrimage with Jesus. Blending his insights from the world of science and religion, and experience forged in the crucible of his personal walk, he highlights the dangers of following received wisdom, clinging on to discredited models, formulas, as well as false and unhelpful dichotomies. He calls us to unlearn bad habits in prayer, and embrace fresh perspectives; with the assurance that God is still in the business of answering prayers.*

"He reaffirms the biblical truth that God is God. He does as He chooses. He is the God of continuity as well as discontinuity. Therefore, science, which is descriptive rather than prescriptive, does not rule out miracles that God performs in response to prayer. It cannot define, restrict, prescribe or determine for God.

"We are invited to walk the walk of faith through the corridor of uncertainty, the pathway of vulnerability and the foggy lane of confusion, grappling with the challenges of answered prayer. The reader is called upon to constantly seek to have a bigger picture of the true and living God who is great and awesome, and ditch the personalised designer gods that we have created for ourselves. We are to think big about God, pray big, and expect big. The one who prays should not seek to box God in as to how He should answer. Because He is God it is His prerogative to respond in a multiplicity of ways to our prayers.

"Last but by no means least; we are challenged to get into partnership with God. He should be the primary focus of our prayer. As He draws us into closer intimacy, His overriding purpose is to change us, make us look like Jesus. Radical transformation is God's chief aim for us when we pray. His desire is to change the world around us, as well as the one who prays, recalibrating our perspective and realigning our will in line with His; leading us to echo these words, 'Your kingdom come, your will be done on earth as it is heaven'.

"This book has encouraged, challenged and informed my thinking and practice on various aspects of my personal prayer life. I wholeheartedly commend it to the humble seeker after truth who desires to grow in their prayer walk with God."

Rev Emmanuel Mbakwe, National Leader, The Apostolic Church UK

Also by David Wilkinson:

God, Time and Stephen Hawking (Monarch, 2001)
Creation: The Bible Speaks Today Bible Themes Series (IVP, 2002)
Christian Eschatology and the Physical Universe (T&T Clark, 2010)
Science, Religion and the Search for Extraterrestrial Life (OUP, 2013)

WHEN I PRAY WHAT DOES GOD DO?

David Wilkinson

MONARCH
BOOKS

Oxford UK, and Grand Rapids, USA

Published by Monarch Books
an imprint of
Lion Hudson plc
Wilkinson House, Jordan Hill Road,
Oxford OX2 8DR, England
Email: monarch@lionhudson.com
www.lionhudson.com/monarch

ISBN 978 0 85721 604 5
e-ISBN 978 0 85721 605 2

First edition 2015

Acknowledgments

Scripture quotations taken from the NIV.
Anglicised. Copyright © 1979, 1984, 2011 Biblica, formerly International
Bible Society. Used by permission of Hodder & Stoughton Ltd, an Hachette
UK company. All rights reserved. "NIV" is a registered trademark of Biblica.
UK trademark number 1448790.
Extract pp. 42–43: Taken from *Finding Organic Church* by Frank Viola
copyright © 2009 Frank Viola. *Finding Organic Church* is published by David
C Cook. All rights reserved.
Extract p. 52: Taken from *The Lion, the Witch and the Wardrobe* by C.S. Lewis
copyright © C.S. Lewis Pte. Ltd. 1950. Extract reprinted by permission.
Extract pp. 53–54: Taken from "Bad Prayer Day?" by Lynda Lee Schab
copyright © 2005 Lynda Lee Schab. Used by permission.
Extract p. 119: Taken from *Miracles* by C.S. Lewis copyright © C.S. Lewis Pte.
Ltd. 1947, 1960. Extract reprinted by permission.
Extract pp. 130–131: Taken from "Cosmology, Ontology, and the Travail
of Biblical Language" by Langdon B. Gilkey copyright © 1961 Langdon B.
Gilkey. Reprinted by permission of The University of Chicago Press.
Extract p. 133: Taken from "Great is Thy Faithfulness" by Thomas O.
Chisholm © 1923. Ren. 1951 Hope Publishing Company, Carol Stream, IL
60188, www.hopepublishing.com. All rights reserved. Used by permission.
Extract pp. 151–152: Taken from *The Two Cultures and a Second Look* by C.P.
Snow copyright © 1969 C.P. Snow. Reprinted by permission of Cambridge
University Press.

A catalogue record for this book is available from the British Library

Printed and bound in the UK, July 2015, LH26

For students and staff, past and present, of
Cranmer Hall and the Wesley Study Centre, whose
commitment to and faithfulness in prayer has
inspired me

Contents

Foreword

T hank heavens for David Wilkinson! It isn't often that theologians who are scientists by training have the courage to ask basic and challenging questions about what we think happens when we pray.

David Wilkinson has no such qualms. In this deeply illuminating and highly accessible book, he tackles directly the fundamental question, "When I pray, what does God do?"

Bringing together his experience as a scientist, theologian, minister and college Principal, he explains that much of our current understanding of God's response to our prayers is diminished. This is because it is based on over-simplistic interpretations of the Bible, reliance on popular myths, and use of outdated scientific models. And most of us, without realising it, have behaved "atheistically" when it comes to the question "When I pray, what does God do?"

David Wilkinson challenges us instead both to be more critical but also more humble in our approach to prayer. He does this first by showing what God actually does do in the Bible. Then in two masterly chapters he explores how current developments in science, especially quantum physics, provide us with new ways of understanding how God can and does respond to our prayers today.

At the same time, David Wilkinson deepens our sense of humility and awe that God is able to act in ways far greater than we can imagine.

This book is a rich resource which will be of great help to both Christians and also to those who feel called to pray but have asked the question, '"When I pray, what goes God do?". David Wilkinson has helped to provide the answer and I highly commend his book to you.

> And Jesus said, "Pray then in this way: Our Father in heaven, hallowed be your name. Your kingdom come. Your will be done, on earth as it is in heaven. Give us this day our daily bread. And forgive us our debts, as we also have forgiven our debtors. And do not bring us to the time of trial, but rescue us from the evil one."
>
> Matthew 6: 9–13

Dr John Sentamu, Archbishop of York

Acknowledgments

There are so many people who have influenced my prayer life and thinking about prayer. In addition, there are many folk who pray for me, my work, and our family regularly and sometimes without our knowing. To write anything on prayer, I have a sense of gratitude to all these people who know more about prayer than I will ever know.

However, there are a few people who have shaped in particular the thinking of this book. Bishop John Pritchard, Bishop Robert Solomon, Dr Ben Witherington, and Revd Professor John Polkinghorne have all written excellent pieces on prayer from which I have learnt and no doubt stolen much! I also owe a great debt to my distinguished predecessor as Principal of St John's College, Dr Ruth Etchells, whose books on prayer and her own life of prayer have been such an inspiration not only to me but to generations of Christians.

Some of the material was developed from an earlier book, *Thinking Clearly About God and Science*, written with my mentor and friend, Rob Frost. Sir Arnold Wolfendale FRS, in a long friendship and then series of discussions and debates, has always asked the difficult questions which so many other people are afraid to ask. Likewise my daughter Hannah's zeal for truth and justice is both inspiring and challenging. Students in the Department of Theology and Religion, Cranmer Hall, and the Wesley Study Centre in Durham encountered some of this material in lectures and refined it by their questions. Other young people, especially at seminars at Soul Survivor and Momentum, likewise pushed some of my own questions further.

I was especially struck by hearing of the approach of my son Adam Wilkinson and his colleague Aaron Routledge on the subject of prayer at The Junction Church Aberdeen, not least on the way they reflected on suffering and unanswered prayer.

I am thankful that the manuscript has been shaped for the better by Tony Collins, Julie Frederick and Jenny Ward at Monarch.

And finally my wife, Alison, whose spirituality and ministry in the midst of illness has given me one of the most holy examples of Christian life and prayer.

CHAPTER 1

My Problems with Prayer

The great twentieth-century preacher Martyn Lloyd-Jones once commented, "Everything we do in the Christian life is easier than prayer." I remember when I first heard this quote and wondering whether I really agreed with it. Is prayer harder than delivering Christian Aid envelopes to a house which has a notice above the letterbox saying "no religious people welcome", accompanied by the sound of a dog whose bark can only come from a hound from hell? Or is prayer harder than a church council meeting where half an hour has been wasted on an argument on the colour of the new mugs for the church hall? Or is prayer harder than trying to understand – and then preach – a sermon on the Trinitarian nature of God?

Surely prayer is one of the easiest parts of the Christian life. It can be done alone, at my own time, in my own space, and after all it is simply a quiet chat with God. Sharing my faith with other people makes me vulnerable to being mocked as a member of the "God-squad". Living as part of a Christian community has its struggles as well as its joys, meaning that I need to love the person whose musical tastes are very different to mine and whose politics will never be even close to mine. Surely, compared to these things, prayer is the simple part of the Christian life.

I used to believe that prayer was easy, although it did strike me that if it was that easy, then why did I not pray more? The problem with prayer, I concluded, was that I simply had not found the right form that suited me. And the history of my prayer life has therefore resembled a Google-like super-spiritual search of different ways of praying. I have tried praying kneeling, standing, sitting, walking, lying down, and crouched in that nonconformist way that everyone in a nonconformist church conforms to. I have prayed with my arms in the air, but with some uncertainty – due to what seems to me to be a change between charismatic generations – about whether I should have my palms up or down! Otherwise, I have prayed with my hands clasped together, with prayer beads and crosses in my hands, and with my arms relaxed and open because someone told me that this welcomes the Holy Spirit. I have prayed for other people with my hands hovering over them just as the charismatic leader John Wimber used to do – until I discovered that there was nothing mystical in this, but simply that Wimber used to pray for folk in a building that was stiflingly hot and had no air conditioning. The hovering laying on of hands was simply to stop it becoming a very sweaty form of ministry. I have prayed with a loud voice and prayed in silence. I have used prayers and liturgies from Christian tradition, prayed in tongues, and used hymns and songs as a form of prayer. I have prayed in prayer meetings, cathedrals, in a small hole in the side of a mountain, on high streets and in convents, and prayed aloud at the same time as 10,000 other people. I have used a prayer journal, prayer cards, prayer letters, and web resources. I have tried praying in the morning, lunchtime, dinnertime, and last thing at night.

All of these forms have been useful – apart from, that is, praying early in the morning! I am the type of person who simply doesn't understand why the Lord created mornings. I am sure that in the Garden of Eden the day started with mid-morning coffee and early mornings are surely the result of the fall!

Nevertheless, for all the diverse exploration of the forms of prayer, I am left with the reality that Lloyd-Jones was right and I actually do find prayer the hardest thing in the Christian life. Why should that be? Perhaps it is to do not with *how I pray* but why I pray and, further, the way that I think about *how God answers prayers.*

Lightning bolts and bishops

Over thirty years ago, in 1984, I was a student at Durham University. I had become a Christian three years previously and, having just completed a physics degree, was about to embark on research in theoretical astrophysics. It was also the time of press interest in the then Bishop of Durham David Jenkins.

Controversy had surrounded his questioning of the traditional interpretations of the virgin birth and the resurrection, with the often misquoted remark linking Bishop David to saying that the resurrection is "a conjuring trick with bones". In fact, the actual quote is a little more difficult to track down, and it is clear that he was trying to say that the resurrection was not *just* a conjuring trick with bones.

The media were further interested in that three days after the bishop's consecration at York Minster, the building was hit by lightning. The subsequent fire in the thirteenth-century south transept left its roof destroyed. Papers picked this up and likened it to the bolt of fire in the story of Elijah and the prophets of Baal. It raised the question of whether this was an act of God's judgment on a bishop with unorthodox views, and indeed whether in a world of modern science we could believe in a God who could work in this kind of way. Bishop David followed all of this up by speaking of how he could not believe in a "laser beam" God who responded to particular prayers by specific acts in the world, picking out one situation to change but leaving so many others.

While having very different views on the virgin birth and resurrection of Jesus, I nevertheless had a great deal of sympathy for the bishop. First of all, I do not think that the fire in York was a sign of God's judgment. I can think of more telling ways if judgment did have to be exercised! Second, Bishop David was attempting to communicate Christian faith in a world often dominated by science. He was an evangelist and a pastor as well as a theologian, and he felt by talking about how traditional belief could be reinterpreted, it would be more accessible to the vast majority of the British public who had rejected faith. He was courageous in publicly stating some of the issues that we all encounter if we want to believe in the existence and power of a God who invites us to pray and then is prepared to answer that prayer.

However, as a young research student it seemed to me that there was a problem in Bishop David's view of science and his view of the Bible. It seemed to me that they were both outdated and somewhat simplistic, and yet I understood completely where they came from.

The predictable world of science

While Bishop David was attempting to find a way to hold together science and Christian belief as a bishop in the public sphere, I was doing exactly the same but privately and as a young research student in astrophysics. This had its own struggles and joys. Science is a messy activity, a long way from school physics where if you do not know the shape of the graph that comes from your experimental data, you simply borrow the book of a person in the year above you who did the same experiment twelve months ago. The struggle for me was trying to make sense of a seemingly mysterious universe, with a limited amount of experimental data, while collaborating with students and staff and also competing against other groups that wanted to get there first. Yet, the joy of science was that it disclosed a universe with beautiful, elegant, and universal laws which applied equally to me dropping a glass and to matter falling into a black hole.

The question was whether in such a universe God had any room at all to answer prayer? It was a question that people often posed to me when they knew I was a scientist. Did I believe that God could intervene in a universe that was governed by the laws of science?

This is not a new question. It goes right back to the scientific revolution, which was in some significant way based on Christian theology and proved both fruitful and challenging for Christian belief. A faithful God, who created the universe freely and yet with a constant commitment to sustaining it, provided the seedbed for the growth of what we know as science. Of course, science stemmed from the Greeks, with notable contributions from Chinese and Muslim thinkers, but the belief in universal and reliable laws which could be discovered by observation was provided by the Christian doctrine of creation. Christians believed that if God was free to create as he wanted, not constrained by human logic, then the only way to see what he had done was to look at the universe. And if God was faithful, our observations would have regularities or patterns to them – that is, the laws of physics. This scientific revolution led to such triumphs as Newton's law of gravitation, which, when coupled with Kepler's elliptical orbits, explains beautifully the movement of the planets around the sun. Such regular and predictable laws of nature could be visualized not only through simple mathematical equations but also in models which represented these motions as a clockwork mechanism. Thus, from the eighteenth century onwards, you could obtain an orrery, a clockwork mechanical model of the solar system that shows the relative positions and motions of the planets (and moons), in their orbits around the sun.

Thus, with a knowledge of the laws of physics and the present position of things, you could tell what had gone on in the past and what was to happen in the future. Edmond Halley's prediction of the arrival of the comet which now bears his name was evidence of how powerful this method was.

The beauty, regularity, and simplicity of the scientific laws were seen as reflections of the order and faithfulness of the creator God. Christian thinkers built on this to try to use the laws to demonstrate the existence of a divine creator. But this in itself led to problems. If everything could be explained by scientific laws, where was there space for God to do anything unusual? If God was a perfect creator then surely he would have built a universe where there is no need for constant intervention in response to prayer. If, after all, I buy an expensive Rolex (in my dreams!) I do not want to be going back to the shop every day asking for it to be fixed. Prayer in this kind of picture either becomes God as the repairman constantly coming to look after faulty equipment, or God as a patronizing adult listening to a child's endless prattling, knowing that everything has been decided already.

The predictable world of charismatic renewal

Yet while I saw the difficulty that science was presenting, I was at the same time growing as a Christian within a culture that accepted that God really did answer prayer. I had become a Christian just before going to university. While brought up in the church, faith only became real to me in the early 1980s.

I had missed the early days of charismatic renewal in the 1960s and 1970s which had sometimes split churches on questions of healing, prophecy, or speaking in tongues. In fact, I remember my interview as a prospective student at Durham, where the college senior tutor, seeing that I was a Christian, warned me against joining the Christian Union. He recounted the story of a group from the Christian Union just a few years before who had felt God had told them not to revise for final exams but to go into the exams and simply pray for the answers. The result was in no way miraculous but very predictable. While their answers were somewhat entertaining in a toe-curling embarrassing way, God apparently refused to be the ultimate exam cheat.

Nevertheless, I did join the Christian Union, feeling that I was far more mature than this previous generation of students. Indeed, most Christians of this evangelical generation found the thought that God might work in miraculous ways quite natural and normal. I did meet a few fellow students who believed that the way God worked in unusual ways in the Old Testament and New Testament was a special dispensation – that is, an unusual time for the beginnings of preaching the gospel – but was not normative for today. Yet I could never see that in the teaching of the Bible, or my experience of student groups, or the churches I attended both during and out of university term.

If a fellow Christian was ill I was very happy to pray for healing and saw some modest apparent answers to such prayer. For example, one friend with diagnosed conjunctivitis seemed to be healed during a five-minute prayer time. I remained sceptical of what I saw as excessive claims of healing but nevertheless felt that the God I read about in the pages of the Bible was ready to respond to prayer in miraculous ways today. At times, in student groups we would be encouraged to write down what requests had been made of God, and to tick them off when such prayers were answered. It is a practice that I do informally in my own prayer life right up to the present, although a friend who did this for his church prayer meeting found an increasing reluctance of people to pray aloud in the meeting!

This was also the belief far from the Christian "hothouse" of my student days. The Methodist church that I grew up in had a weekly prayer meeting, and during the vacations I was one of the six or seven people who were the regular attenders. This prayer meeting had been going a long time and was somewhat predictable in the order of who prayed and how we prayed. Most prayers were prefaced with "Lord, if it be your will". In fact, a story was often told of a prayer meeting during the Second World War at this church where someone had prayed,

"Lord, we pray for complete victory for Britain over Hitler and his armies, but Lord, if it is not your will, then please let it be a draw!" The range of subjects for prayer included those in the church who were ill, but it also regularly included prayer for peace in Northern Ireland and the ending of apartheid in South Africa. Here was always the expectation that God would answer prayer in the big issues of life and death, in our community and on the world stage.

This was the normal Christian life as far as I was concerned. I noted some of the scientific problems with this expectation that God would answer such prayers, but did not really engage with questions of how God did it. I suppose at times it was enough to hold to a view that I would later learn was called "NOMA" by Stephen Jay Gould (1941–2002) – that is, the non-overlapping magisteriums of science and religion. Gould, attempting to head off the battles of science and religion in US education, argued that science had its own territory and so did religion, but the two would never meet. The scientist was a scientist Monday to Saturday in the laboratory and a person of faith on a Sunday.

This was an easy option to fall into, but deep down I was not satisfied with it. It seemed to me that if I proclaimed Jesus as Lord he needed to be Lord not only of my heart but also my mind, of my Bible reading and my work as a scientist, of Sunday and of Monday morning. To live in two worlds, as a charismatic Christian believing God would answer prayer and a practising scientist believing that God was the source of the wonderful scientific laws, was not sufficient for Jesus as Lord. I needed to at least keep asking the question of how God answered prayer, even if I might never get a full and satisfying answer.

Yet there was another problem for prayer that was and is more serious than the scientific one.

The seemingly unpredictable and trivial will of God

I have heard many Christian friends speak of how God has answered prayers on issues that seem to me to be a trivial waste of God's time: "I prayed for a parking space in the supermarket and immediately a car pulled out and I could pull straight in." I had a friend once who crashed his car while he was praying. Fortunately no one was injured, but he still has to endure the jokes about whether he had his hands in the air or whether he had his eyes closed!

Far more serious is the question of why God chooses to answer such trivial questions rather than answer some of the more important questions. Why produce a parking space for a Christian who could probably benefit from a little walk by parking further away rather than heal the person who is going through excruciating pain?

I have prayed for the healing of others throughout my Christian life, sometimes in my own prayer life, sometimes sitting beside them, and sometimes from the front of churches. I have seen some remarkable things. Elsie was a member of a church where I was a pastor, and a colleague and I were called to her hospital bedside after a stroke and told she would not make it through the night. We prayed for God to be with her and to heal her, although fully expecting that her time in this life was now at an end. After sitting with her for some considerable time during the night we eventually left to get some rest, again expecting that we would receive a phone call the next day from the hospital and the undertakers. Next morning, when there had been no phone call, we returned to the hospital to find her sitting up in bed having lunch. Within a few weeks she was back up on her feet serving other elderly people at our weekly luncheon club. To say that the doctors and nurses were surprised was an understatement, but not as surprised as we were! Now of course it is difficult to say that this was solely an answer to prayer. The mind/brain connection as we will see in a later chapter is mysterious, and the ability for the brain to find new pathways around damaged areas is remarkable. It may have been that well-meaning hospital staff had erred on the side of caution in warning of her imminent death. Maybe she would have recovered anyway without our prayer.

If such instances of healing are puzzling, far more difficult are the occasions when I have prayed earnestly and felt full of faith, but the person has not been healed. This is especially the case when the person concerned seems so deserving or is very close to you.

When unanswered prayer is personal

My wife Alison is a brilliant Methodist minister. For twelve years she served a church just outside Durham and transformed it from an elderly and rather traditional church into a church of all ages with lots of new initiatives – prayer meetings, Christmas and Easter journeys for local schools, Messy Church, Café Church, a group for 20s–30s, a group for teenagers, the sponsoring of a large number of children in developing countries, and new ways of engaging with the Bible. As a church we were blessed by her ministry of preaching and leading. Yet, over the past eight years she has been literally struck down with two major illnesses.

The first occurred immediately after preaching at a youth celebration. She returned to the house on the Sunday evening feeling unwell and by the Monday morning had become very ill. It was a form of ME or chronic fatigue which was so severe that initially she lost the ability to talk and to move. In fact, the doctors were so worried that she was sent for a brain scan in case it was a tumour. Thankfully, it was not a tumour, but the condition had its own challenges. While it seems to be caused by the body's immune system malfunctioning, there is widespread disagreement in the medical community about its specific cause and its treatment. It is a difficult condition to understand, both for the person going through it and for those around. Well-intentioned people give advice from "cut this out of your diet" to "pull yourself together" to "God will heal you". For a period Alison could not preach or indeed

27

work as a church leader. The church, growing so quickly, had to manage without its minister. Alison prayed, our children and I prayed, and the church prayed. Many of us could not understand why these things happen and why God did not provide miraculous healing.

Over months she gradually recovered and was nearing full fitness when she began to experience pain in her joints. Referred to a physiotherapist, this treatment only made the pain worse. Eventually she was diagnosed with rheumatoid arthritis, an incurable and progressive disease which is the immune system attacking the joints. Although better understood, treatment is not straightforward, featuring a trial and error process with families of drugs, some of which take three to six months to make a difference or to assess their effectiveness. It is a disease which causes intense pain and intense weariness, and for some eighteen months again Alison was unable to work in the church. Again we all prayed, but there was no miraculous cure. Only recently, a combination of drugs and Alison's ability to work around the disease has allowed her to get back to work part-time – but she is limited in so many ways and still in constant pain.

We both remember, in the light of this, a prayer said by a dear friend at our wedding. We had asked a number of people to come and pray with us during the service, and our friend had prayed that our life together would be blessed with good health. Yet like many other families, we have had to cope with a fair share of illness over the years. Did God simply ignore this prayer?

The additional factor is that Alison has been involved in such key work for God's kingdom, and because of her role she has had so many people praying for her health – this intensifies the difficult questions concerning prayer.

The obvious question in all of this is, what *is* God doing in answer to the many prayers being said? The question is so much more serious when you see a person you love suffering. This is a far more difficult problem than that of the scientific laws in trying to understand how God works in answer to prayer, for it questions not just God's ability but also God's will to change the world for good.

The problem with the God of the Bible

If science and suffering both pose really difficult questions to how God answers prayer, the Bible does not give clear and simple answers. This is because it is not written in this way. The Bible does not have a subject index, it does not address philosophical questions in a systematic way, and it does not have any intention of doing so.

Of course, there are now numerous websites that try to do this for you. I came across one the other day which offered the Bible's view on subjects as diverse as hunting, the wearing of T-shirts with slogans, pyramid schemes (financial rather than burial!), and war in the Middle East. I was intrigued, wondering which verse in the Bible gave me guidance on whether I should wear a T-shirt with the slogan "Keep calm and carry on". Of course, to be fair to the website, clicking on one of these subjects took you to quite an extended essay where biblical principles were applied to each of these questions rather than a single verse which gave a succinct answer. This lack of easy short answers in the Bible is frustrating not only to the person who wants to write a book on prayer, but also to the person who is simply wanting a quick answer to how God answers prayer.

Yet the Bible understood in the Christian tradition is much more interesting, exciting, and important than just a long "Frequently asked questions" appendix to the concept of God. It is the record of God's self-revelation through his acts in history, covering large time periods, various cultural contexts, and relationship with individuals, groups, and nations. It is a divinely inspired and God-breathed collection of sixty-six different books featuring a wide spectrum of different types of literature. Some of this literature, such as the book of Romans, does provide a carefully constructed logical argument on a particular aspect of how God deals with human beings. But there are other genres in the Bible, the purpose of which is not logical argument but stories to draw us deeper into relationship with the God of the Bible. So the parables of Jesus give us insight into the kingdom of God which we need to live with and struggle with on the journey of being a disciple. Therefore, the Bible's teaching on prayer comes in lots of different places and sometimes in exhortation, sometimes in story, and sometimes in example.

The biblical writers are united in their encouragement to see the importance of prayer and its centrality in the Christian life. Thus Paul writes in 1 Thessalonians, "Rejoice always, pray continually, give thanks in all circumstances; for this is God's will for you in Christ Jesus" (5:16–18).

However, when we get to asking the question about how God responds to prayer we encounter a number of pictures which do not fit into a simple pattern. Prayer is likened to a child–parent relationship, but it is also likened to a persistent widow and a rather dodgy judge (Luke 11:2; 18:1–8). The prayer of a righteous person is commended as having great effect, and yet God seems to answer the prayers of people with myopic understanding, frail faith, and questionable lifestyle. At times God seems to respond directly to a person's prayer in seemingly changing his mind and direction of action, and at other times seems to a weave a person's prayer into a narrative which already knows its end. Much to our modern frustration, questions of unjust suffering are rarely explored and never in the philosophical terms we would prefer. Thus the book of Job through story and dialogue shows the inadequacy of many simplistic answers to suffering and leads us into a new encounter with the living God of creation. In a similar way, God's special and unusual actions are presented alongside his constant sustaining of the universe without any exploration of the relationship between these two things.

Over the years I have come to accept and embrace this nature of the biblical account. I am an evangelical Christian and that means that for me the Bible is supreme in all matters of faith and conduct. But the problem of evangelical Christianity has often been to exalt certain doctrinal formulas above the authority of the Scriptures themselves. Rather for me, it is a matter of constantly going back to the richness of the Bible and living under it. One of my great heroes, the Baptist preacher Dr Alan Redpath, once said it is great when you go to the Bible, tap it with a silver hammer, and it falls into three neat pieces – the basis of a sermon! But, he said, it is far more powerful when the Bible takes your pride, expectations, and inadequate understandings and breaks you into pieces!

While the multi-genre and multi-purpose nature of the Bible poses problems to understanding how God responds to prayer, perhaps the real "problem" of the biblical God is the one thing that is stated clearly and unambiguously across all the different genres of Scripture – that is, God is the one who answers prayers. As we shall see, some of the options to avoid the problems of science and suffering are to remove the possibility that God actually does something in response to prayer. Prayer can be seen as thanksgiving, confession, and meditation on God's goodness. It certainly is that, but the biblical writers see it as more than that. Intercession and petition – that is, asking God to do something in response to prayer – is unashamedly presented and encouraged in the Bible. This may seem an obvious point but it can easily be lost in theological discussion. It is worth just giving a flavour of this from the biblical writers:

*Isaac prayed to the Lord on behalf of his wife, because she
was childless. The Lord answered his prayer, and his wife
Rebekah became pregnant.*

Genesis 25:21

*They buried the bones of Saul and his son Jonathan in the
tomb of Saul's father Kish, at Zela in Benjamin, and did
everything the king commanded. After that, God answered
prayer on behalf of the land.*

2 Samuel 21:14

*David built an altar to the Lord there and sacrificed burnt
offerings and fellowship offerings. Then the Lord answered
his prayer on behalf of the land, and the plague on Israel
was stopped.*

2 Samuel 24:25

*They were helped in fighting them, and God delivered
the Hagrites and all their allies into their hands, because
they cried out to him during the battle. He answered their
prayers, because they trusted in him.*

1 Chronicles 5:20

*So we fasted and petitioned our God about this, and he
answered our prayer.*

Ezra 8:23

You who answer prayer, to you all people will come.

Psalm 65:2

*"Go and tell Hezekiah, 'This is what the Lord, the God of
your father David, says: I have heard your prayer and seen
your tears; I will add fifteen years to your life.'"*

Isaiah 38:5

But the angel said to him: "Do not be afraid, Zechariah;
your prayer has been heard. Your wife Elizabeth will bear
you a son, and you are to call him John."

Luke 1:13

His father was sick in bed, suffering from fever and
dysentery. Paul went in to see him and, after prayer, placed
his hands on him and healed him.

Acts 28:8

One cannot read these passages without being struck with the knowledge that this is a God who, in the experience of the biblical writers, acts in the physical world and answers prayer. For Christians, our supreme revelation of the nature of God is in Jesus. Jesus matches his teaching on prayer with his example of prayer, praying at times alone and at times with his disciples. And his teaching is clear that part of the relationship that he makes possible with the Father comes with the invitation to ask:

"Ask and it will be given to you; seek and you will find;
knock and the door will be opened to you. For everyone who
asks receives; the one who seeks finds; and to the one who
knocks, the door will be opened.

"Which of you, if your son asks for bread, will give him
a stone? Or if he asks for a fish, will give him a snake? If
you, then, though you are evil, know how to give good gifts
to your children, how much more will your Father in heaven
give good gifts to those who ask him!"

Matthew 7:7–11

And yet I still pray...

Even in our scientific and increasingly secular Western world, prayer continues to be practised widely. Surveys show that 75 to 97 per cent of Americans claimed that they pray once a week and 57 per cent one or more times a day.[1] In fact, the proportion of people who pray has remained the same in the US over a time period of forty years, although the frequency has declined.[2] A 1997 *Newsweek* survey reported that 87 per cent of Americans agreed that "God answers prayers" and 82 per cent said that when praying they "ask for health or success for a child or family member". In another survey conducted by Gallup, three in ten Americans reported a "remarkable healing", of whom 30 per cent linked this healing to their own or other people's prayers.

I understand this. My own personal experience of science and, to a lesser extent, suffering makes me question a whole number of aspects of prayer and how God answers. However, my experience of God in the Bible and in my daily life continues to encourage me to pray expectantly that God will act. But this, I hope, is not because I simply live in two different worlds, shutting out the difficult questions by immersing myself in loud choruses and sheltering in a bubble of Christian subculture.

---

1   General Social Survey 2008; Bader, C., Dougherty, K., Froese, P., Johnson, B., Mencken, F. C., Park, J., et al. (2006). *American Piety in the 21st Century: New Insights to the Depth and Complexity of Religion in the US: Selected Findings from the Baylor Religion Survey.* Waco, TX: Baylor Institute for Studies of Religion.
2   Poloma, M. M. and Gallup, G. H., Jr (1991). *Varieties of Prayer: A Survey Report.* Philadelphia: Trinity Press International.

I continue to pray because, as I have struggled with the difficult questions, I have learnt and am still learning some valuable lessons into how God might act in response to prayer. This has not been one overarching and simple explanation, but rather a kaleidoscope of insights which sometimes form coherent patterns and sometimes are somewhat chaotic.

This book is an attempt to share those insights. First, I have learnt to identify and reject some unhelpful views of God derived from popular views on how God answers prayer. This is the area explored in Chapter 2, where I suggest that it is easy to slip into bad theology and this has a long-term negative consequence for prayer. Chapter 3 goes back to the Bible to suggest that the biblical material is far more complex on prayer than we often acknowledge. Here it is important to look at specific incidents in their own contexts, rather than the usual approach, which is to "flatten out" the biblical complexity by synthesizing themes across the whole of the Bible. By taking Scripture seriously, we can fruitfully engage in the complexity of life and the complexity of the question of how God works in response to prayer. Chapters 4 and 5 explore my particular interest in how science impacts this question, arguing that the scientific ideas which proved so detrimental to belief in prayer and God acting in unusual ways in the universe are now outdated. New understandings of the natural world in quantum theory and chaos do not give an easy solution to how God works, but they do give possibilities and, more importantly, challenge the way that pre-twentieth-century science has been used in theology. I find these understandings exciting and encouraging in my own prayer life. Chapter 6 attempts to bring together into some kind of pattern the biblical, scientific, and practical ideas which help me have some understanding of how God answers prayer and what that means for my own prayer life. This is far from a perfect pattern, and many questions – not least the problem of unjust suffering – remain unanswered.

This book is not an attempt to provide a definitive answer to how God answers prayer. It is more a record of a personal and an ongoing journey of how a Christian who wants to take both the Bible and science seriously begins to think about these things.

CHAPTER 2

Everyday Myths of Prayer

"The problem with prayer is other Christians," a friend once remarked to me. She was referring to her dislike of prayer meetings and her preference for more solitary prayer. However, it seems to me that there is a deeper sense of the problem. The writer on Christian renewal and the history of revival, Richard Lovelace, once observed, "One person's piety is another person's poison." That's the trouble with books on prayer and advice from other Christians, even those whose understanding and practice of prayer has been outstanding.

The eager person wanting to learn about prayer is often an uncritical sponge who soaks up any insight or prejudice about prayer. I have often been like that myself. We all want desperately to be better at prayer and therefore any model which seems to work well is in danger of being uncritically adopted. The trouble is that the odd quote or anecdote, the section of a sermon or extract from a book, can certainly encourage, but can also become a massive burden. The burden comes from trying to reproduce the practice from one person to another, or, more seriously, pick up a corrupted view of the nature of God and God's response to prayer.

For example, the amazing growth of the South Korean megachurches has attracted a lot of interest from Western Christians wanting to reproduce such growth in their own congregations. One of the striking features of the Korean churches has been early morning prayer meetings, some starting at 5 a.m. during the working week. I know a number of enthusiastic British pastors who tried to recreate the pattern, exhorting their people to see this as being the way forward. The results were often discouraging for the pastors when they were the only ones there at 5 a.m., and for the congregations who felt immensely guilty for not being able to show enough Christian commitment to achieve what Alan Redpath used to call "duvet victory". Of course anyone who has visited Seoul will know that prayer meetings are not the only things going on in the early hours of the morning. The day starts much earlier for most people, and the nature of work and rest is very different from that of, say, Sunderland! Yet it is very easy to give the impression that if we are not all up and praising the Lord at 5 a.m. then churches will never grow. And is God the kind of God who only hears early morning prayer rather than late at night prayer? The important principle to learn from the Korean church is about the centrality of prayer and to adapt its practice into a different culture, rather than to attempt an exact copy.

The first book I read on prayer was a small booklet called *The Power of Prayer* by E. M. Bounds, and to be honest I never quite recovered from it. Bounds reviewed the prayer lives of the great saints of Christian tradition in order to encourage other Christians to do the same. The trouble was that I found it discouraging rather than encouraging. For example, Martin Luther, if he had a particularly busy day, would say, "Tomorrow I plan to work; work, from early until late. In fact I have so much to do that I shall spend the first three hours in prayer." Now, I didn't take from this the insight that all work for God has to be embedded in prayer; instead, I felt guilty about my inability to spend anything like thirty minutes, rather than three hours, in prayer. Further, I took the subtle sense that unless I was spending hours in prayer then God would not answer my prayers. It is interesting that I could have made such a mistake from such a quote. Luther himself of course stressed that salvation was not earned by good deeds but was the free gift of God's grace through Jesus Christ. God's favour was not dependent on my commitment, not even my commitment in prayer.

Of course, there is much I have received from the insights of fellow Christians, although it is fair to say that I have learnt the most from those who have admitted their weaknesses rather than shared their strengths in prayer. However, more significant, in its influence for both good and bad, is not what fellow Christians say, write, or preach, but what fellow Christians do. There is a subtle subculture to the Christian church where ideas of God and answers to prayer are embedded in hymns, songs, public prayers, and the practice of leadership. As a child I was always interested in the custom among many of the Methodist preachers that during the hymn before the sermon they would stop singing and curl up behind the pulpit in fervent prayer. I wondered what they were doing – was this prayer needed for the sermon, for them, or for us as the congregation? Was it directing the congregation's attention to God or marking out the preacher as someone who was holier than the rest of us? And from the standard of some of the sermons that followed, it did seem to me to be a waste of time!

I was also intrigued by other practices. Why do some Christians come into church before worship and bow their heads in prayer, and then after the service the first thing before the rush for chocolate biscuits and coffee is another bow of the head? Does God have some mystical system for clocking in and clocking out for worship? And why do some Christians preface every prayer with "Lord we just…"?

Now I have done all these things and more, for no reason other than I see fellow Christians doing them and the power of pious peer pressure. It is when our subculture starts to mislead us on God that a gentle smile at our shared eccentricities turns to a more worried frown. One of my favourite worship songs rejoices in God being mighty to save but has the line, "he can move the mountains". It is a piece of poetic imagery that can be misleading. Where in the Bible does it say that God can, or wants, to move mountains? Jesus does say, "Truly I tell you, if you have faith as small as a mustard seed, you can say to this mountain, 'Move from here to there,' and it will move. Nothing will be impossible for you" (Matthew 17:20). Later in the same Gospel, he continues, "Truly I tell you, if you have faith and do not doubt, not only can you do what was done to the fig tree, but also you can say to this mountain, 'Go, throw yourself into the sea,' and it will be done" (Matthew 21:21). While there is no doubt an allusion in the song to the effect on the mountain when Moses received the Law in Exodus, there is no record of God actually moving a mountain. One Christian blogger writes, "I know my God can move a mountain. I've seen Him do it many times before and can't wait til I watch Him do it again."[3] When I read this I immediately wanted to see this on YouTube! Now of course she meant it metaphorically and went on to talk about the amazing answers to prayer, but just for a moment my mind was filled with the literal image – how did God do it and what was left behind, and was this a regular occurrence which I had never noticed when driving through the Pennines?

In his book *Finding Organic Church,* Frank Viola notes the way that prayer meetings influence the way we think about God:

> *Many Christians have picked up a great deal of artificiality in the way they pray and talk about spiritual matters. This is largely due to imitating bad models. To be more pointed: The way that many Christians pray is abysmal. I would*

3   http://suzettejones.blogspot.co.uk/2009/02/he-can-move-mountain.html

advise against having meetings where everyone offers a prayer request. Why? Two reasons. First, those meetings will no doubt turn out to be highly religious. (In every "prayer-request" meeting I've ever been in, the kinds of things that some Christians ask God to do for them range from the ludicrous to the insane.) Second, those meetings will be the first step down a slippery slope that will eventually become the death knell for your group. There's a great deal of unlearning and relearning that we Christians need when it comes to communing with the Lord. If the truth be told, most Christians would do well to allow their way of praying to go into death.[4]

I do not agree with such a stark assessment but I do see the point being made. I have always benefited from praying with other people in prayer meetings, but Viola is right in highlighting the danger of picking up bad practice and theology in such settings.

Then there are those of us who pick up, through childhood or through brief contact with Christian faith, concepts that stay with us for years. For some it is the Lord's Prayer, which they understood from an early age as "Our Father who are in heaven, Harold is thy name" or "But deliver us from Mabel". In a similar way, for years I could not understand why in Psalm 23 if the Lord was my shepherd then I should dismiss him with "I shall not want".

---

4   Viola, F. (2009). *Finding Organic Church: A Comprehensive Guide to Starting and Sustaining Authentic Christian Communities*. Colorado Springs: David C. Cook, p. 212.

So whether through misunderstanding, confusion, or just plain wrong teaching, many of us grow up with misleading pictures of God and prayer. They take on the nature of myths, powerful and shaping stories, which in these cases are both unhelpful to prayer and misleading about God. Let's have a look at seven of them, although of course there are many more. In this, we will need to pay attention to the influence and accessibility of the digital environment. While this kind of exercise in the past may have concentrated entirely on books or pamphlets on prayer, today Christian thinking is more readily shaped by the web – for the casual browser can encounter a multitude of web hits on the subject of prayer with a wide variety of theological assumptions.

The "slot machine of faith" God

Many Christians would run a mile from the one-arm bandits of the local amusement arcade, internet gambling, or even the gigantic machines of Las Vegas. Yet often God is presented in such terms. Slot machines draw you in, promising a dramatic life-changing result with the sense that the more money you put in the better chance you have of getting that pay-out. Then, the bigger the machine the more dramatic a win is. One woman who won over £20 million on the Megabucks machine at the Desert Inn in Las Vegas said, "I have been playing Megabucks for several years but I am not a heavy gambler. If you don't try you don't win." While the chance of a win is less on a big machine, the size of the jackpot is much bigger and so people waste a great deal of time and money trying to get the machine to pay out.

There is a view of prayer which is not too far away from this: God can do something dramatic in my life if I pray enough. I know that the chances that God might do something dramatic are very low, but if I put enough faith into the slot and pull the handle of prayer often enough, then I might get lucky.

Such a view of God's response to prayer has a number of fundamental weaknesses. A slot machine is a mechanical device, with its random nature of giving a pay-out carefully controlled in favour of the casino rather than the gambler. God in this myth is therefore merely a machine whose response to prayer is biased against the person who prays, and any answer comes just from frequency and luck. God is not relational, personal, or on the side of human beings. South African pastor and author Andrew Murray once observed, "Beware in your prayers, above everything else, of limiting God, not only by unbelief, but by fancying that you know what He can do."

It is a myth which also puts us as the person who prays at the centre of it all. We are acting first in prayer so that God then acts in a way that we have asked for. The prayer that results can be quite prescriptive and centred entirely on our own needs. The following prayer, which can be found in many places on the web, makes fun of this understanding of prayer:

Dear Lord,

*Help me to relax about insignificant details, beginning
tomorrow at 7:41:23 a.m. EST.*

*Help me to consider people's feelings, even if most of
them are hypersensitive.*

*Help me to take responsibility for the consequences of my
actions, even though they're usually not my
fault.*

*Help me to not try to run everything – but, if you
need some help, please feel free to ask me.*

*Help me to be more laid back, and help me to do it
exactly right.*

*Help me to take things more seriously, especially
laughter, parties, and dancing.*

Give me patience, and I mean right now!

*Help me not be a perfectionist. (Did I spell that
correctly?)*

Help me to finish everything I sta

*Help me to keep my mind on one thing ... oh, look, a
bird ... at a time.*

*Help me to do only what I can, and trust you for the
rest. And would you mind putting that in writing?*

*Keep me open to others' ideas, misguided though
they may be.*

*Help me follow established procedures. Hey, wait ...
this is wrong ...*

Help me slow down andnotrushthroughwhatido.

Thank you, Lord.

Amen

It is all about me and little about God. But I recognize just how tempting such a view is, and I recognize how often it has been true of my own prayer life. It can also be true of the way churches pray. If there is a major evangelistic outreach coming then we need to have special prayer meetings, as if our chances of success are increased by the amount of prayer we say.

Some will say, "But is there not biblical justification for such an approach?", quoting the parable of the persistent widow from Luke 18:

> *Then Jesus told his disciples a parable to show them that they should always pray and not give up. He said: "In a certain town there was a judge who neither feared God nor cared what people thought. And there was a widow in that town who kept coming to him with the plea, 'Grant me justice against my adversary.'*
>
> *"For some time he refused. But finally he said to himself, 'Even though I don't fear God or care what people think, yet because this widow keeps bothering me, I will see that she gets justice, so that she won't eventually come and attack me!'"*
>
> *And the Lord said, "Listen to what the unjust judge says. And will not God bring about justice for his chosen ones, who cry out to him day and night? Will he keep putting them off? I tell you, he will see that they get justice, and quickly. However, when the Son of Man comes, will he find faith on the earth?"*

So should we just keep bothering God to try to persuade him to get on our side? But the whole point of the parable is that God is much more for us, "his chosen ones", than the cranky and unrighteous judge. The parable leads us to think about not giving up in prayer, rather than the sheer amount of prayer. Even if the circumstances are tough we can go on praying in confidence that if God is for us then who is against us? Too much prayer in a funny kind of way can be symptomatic of a lack of confidence in God's love for us.

The "health and wealth" God

I remember having a conversation with a young Christian woman who was a key member of one of the largest congregations in the world at that time. We were talking about prayer and she was vehement in her belief that if you prayed for healing and financial blessing then God would give that. She pointed to the way that God had blessed her church and her own life in this way. It was a strong argument. When I tried to suggest, however, that God's blessing was not always in health and wealth, then her response was very simple, "So do you think God wants us to be sick and poor?" Deeply embedded in this kind of message is the sense that God wants the best for us and it is just a matter of asking in the right way.

This teaching – sometimes referred to as "health and wealth", and sometimes as the "prosperity gospel" – points to promises in the Bible and sees them as a contract that God will fulfil. It finds its scriptural justification in the interpretation of a few passages, such as John 10:10, "The thief comes only to steal and kill and destroy; I have come that they may have life, and have it to the full", and 2 Corinthians 8:9, "For you know the grace of our Lord Jesus Christ, that though he was rich, yet for your sake he became poor, so that you through his poverty might become rich." It therefore attempts to take the Bible seriously, which is certainly an advantage over the slot machine God.

Yet the verses are interpreted purely in terms of material blessings in this life. It is significant that this movement grew especially in the US in the 1950s, alongside consumerism and the American dream. Happiness in life through health and wealth was the common theme that fuelled advertising, healthcare, technology, industry, and prayer. In this the media played a crucial role. The emergence of television advertising was joined by aspirational programmes taking the viewer into a future dream of what life could really be like. Learning their craft from the communication culture of radio and television, televangelists were at the forefront of the prosperity gospel, promising that God would heal and increase wealth in response to faith – and that faith of course would be demonstrated by a cheque or credit card donation to their ministry. The dominance of American media culture and consumer power effectively exported the prosperity gospel to many different parts of the world. It has found a ready audience in those excluded from health and wealth by political and national structures.

Television advertising promises much, but the experience of consumers is that it rarely delivers. The burger which looks so large and enticing on screen seems to be very much smaller in the drive-through. The popular men's antiperspirant does not seem to attract multitudes of beautiful girls, never mind just how much teenage boys spray it on. Even car insurance is never quite the deal it seems. Experience in prayer can be quite like this. The testimony of Christians on the main stages of conventions or on Christian media never seems to fully resonate with our experience of prayer. The mountains might tremble just a little but never move an inch! It is easy to become disillusioned very quickly, if we have invested our faith, and sometimes our money, in such promises.

The Baptist pastor and author John Piper once commented, "It is not surprising that prayer malfunctions when we try to make it a domestic intercom to call upstairs for more comforts in the den." Indeed, if my wife happens to be in the kitchen and I ask for a cup of tea while I am watching the cricket, then although she loves me I cannot be sure of the response. Sometimes a cup of tea will come, but sometimes there are a range of responses from "we've run out of milk" to "get it yourself, you lazy slob!" As with the slot machine God, believers in the health and wealth gospel expect only one kind of response from God. It also imposes onto the biblical promises a range of assumptions that have very little to do with the original words of Jesus or the early church. Fullness of life in John's Gospel is not about health and wealth but rather about encounter with truth and the life of God in Jesus. To interpret Paul's words of rich and poor in Corinthians in financial terms is simply bizarre. The richness that Jesus gave up for us was not a heavenly bank balance but his close communion with the Father and the honour he had as the Son (Philippians 2:6–8).

However, it is the picture of God which comes out of this that is the most troubling. This kind of teaching was beautifully satirized by Will Ferrell in the 2006 movie *Talladega Nights: The Ballad of Ricky Bobby*. Ferrell plays the title role of a successful NASCAR driver with a stunning wife, children, and mansion. When the family gathers for a meal, Ricky says grace, thanking "baby Jesus" for the family, money, and his winnings. When challenged in the midst of the prayer about his constant reference to baby Jesus, Ricky argues that he prefers the cuddly infant Christmas Jesus to the Easter Jesus. The theological critique, whether meant or not, is spot on. Without the picture of God's love shown in the cross and resurrection, Western culture has merged the baby Jesus with Santa Claus. As long as you are not naughty but nice then presents from God will be on their way.

The "health and wealth" God is an indulgent parent always responding to a child's request as long as they act nicely. Their complete focus is on their child to the exclusion of everything else. But further, the parent is thus fulfilled by wanting to be needed.

The God of the Bible is very different to this picture. He is loving but not indulgent. He takes delight in human beings but does not need to be needed. Because God is good, he is not to be easily manipulated or domesticated to our whims or wishes. C. S. Lewis explored this view of God in the character of Aslan in *The Lion, the Witch and the Wardrobe*. When the children ask Mr Beaver if Aslan is a safe lion, he replies, "Course he isn't safe, but he's good." True prayer encounters this reality of God which is both disturbing and comforting.

The "keep putting money into the meter" God

One of the great insights from many parts of the Christian church is that you grow in prayer by doing it regularly. In my own tradition of evangelical Christianity, the emphasis is on the individual morning quiet time before the work of the day starts. In the Anglican tradition, the office of morning prayer gives prayer a communal setting framed by regular and systematic reading of Scripture. This forms a rhythm to life, worship, and discipleship. In the monastic tradition, different times of the day are marked for prayer, keeping a continual reminder of the presence and power of God.

There is much to be commended in this approach. You see a rhythm of prayer in the life of Jesus and in the early church. Jesus rises early and goes away by himself for prayer (Mark 1:35; Matthew 14:23) and is a regular at the synagogue (Luke 4:16). The disciples post-resurrection meet regularly (Acts 2:42) and there seems to be a constant turning to prayer in times of difficulty (Acts 4:23–31).

Indeed, neuroscience has shown a wide range of practices where a repeated rhythm of actions leads to growth and healing in the mind. For example, people recovering from strokes are encouraged to do regular "drills" to help the brain work around damaged areas. Following a pattern or rhythm of prayer has led many Christians to testify to a heightened sense of the presence of God, healing, and strength in difficult times. I have found this to be true in my own prayer life. I have not adopted the same pattern for the whole of my Christian life, but have experimented with different patterns and changed patterns regularly. However, the importance of a pattern of prayer has been core to knowing God better.

Yet there is a danger in such an approach, which can come out as another myth about God and prayer. It is that you get a feeling that unless you have prayed at the appointed time, then the rest of the day will be a failure because you are living without power. Blogger Lynda Lee Schab likens it to having a bad hair day:

> For me, when my hair looks great, every strand in its place,
> I feel confident, beautiful, and able to conquer the world!
> When it's too flat and just won't do anything at all, my
> morning is off to a bad start. The remainder of the day I feel
> cranky and irritable… I have found something else that
> affects my entire day: a bad prayer day. When I start off
> the day in prayer, I feel confident, a beautiful daughter of
> the King, and everything somehow falls into place. When
> I don't pray at all, or try to squeeze in a quick request

or two between downing a bagel and brushing my teeth,
my morning is already off to a bad start. The remainder
of the day I feel cranky and irritable, frustrated and
discontented… God desires for me to spend time with Him
in prayer every morning, filling up on everything I need to
face the day.[5]

There are some of us, of course, who never have a good hair day, never mind a great prayer day. But the view of a "bad prayer day" can mean not only that you do not feel quite right, but it can also lead to a sense of guilt and a wasted day where you think God will not bless you. In extreme cases you build a picture that because you have missed prayer God has turned his back to you.

Being a heavy sleeper who is not good at all in the mornings, I have always struggled with morning quiet times – both to get up and to get my mind engaged in Bible study and prayer. For years I struggled with this sense of guilt and fear that I had not demonstrated enough spiritual commitment for prayer to be answered.

Yet this image of God is once again mechanical and far from the God of the Bible. It has a sense of if you do a favour for God by praying then he will do a favour for you. We are back to a slot machine God or a contractual God. The God of the Bible is indeed a God who makes covenants with his people, but these covenants always begin with God's freely undeserved favour, his grace. It is only on the basis of this

---

5   http://www.faithwriters.com/article-details.php?id=25242

grace, shown in God's acts, that the people of Israel were called to follow certain obligations in the covenant. Prayer is more than keeping God happy in order that he answers our requests.

The further difficulty of the "keep putting money into the meter" God is that the performance of prayer becomes more about how you look to other people rather than intimate communion with God. In the Sermon on the Mount in Matthew's Gospel, Jesus cautions his disciples about this kind of approach:

> And when you pray, do not be like the hypocrites, for they love to pray standing in the synagogues and on the street corners to be seen by others. Truly I tell you, they have received their reward in full. But when you pray, go into your room, close the door and pray to your Father, who is unseen. Then your Father, who sees what is done in secret, will reward you. And when you pray, do not keep on babbling like pagans, for they think they will be heard because of their many words.
>
> Matthew 6:5–7

I teach in a college which, among many other things, trains men and women for church leadership primarily in the Church of England. It is a requirement of such training that you are at morning prayer each weekday morning and at other times of public prayer and worship during the week. This is an entirely good requirement as it helps to form the pattern of the prayer life of leaders. But I suspect (and indeed know from my own attitudes) that the motivation to be at morning prayer can often be primarily to be seen there by colleagues and staff rather than a delight to read the Scriptures and pray! It is also the case in some prayer meetings that prayers become lengthy in order to demonstrate the holiness and doctrinal soundness of the person who prays.

It is interesting that Jesus couples the warnings about the wrong motivation in prayer with the critique of those who babble "like pagans". It is those who have a wrong view of God who think that he is to be convinced by many words. His blessing is not to be guaranteed or sustained by our prayer. It is there anyway.

When our children were small we once rented a cottage in Scarborough in January for a short break. Scarborough is great during the summer but that winter it was snow, sleet, and record low temperatures. We discovered that the heating worked by putting coins into a slot. It was so cold that we had to go to a bank each morning for a bag of coins and found ourselves feeding coins into the meter so often that we placed an easy chair beside the meter so that one of us could sit beside it. That was before we discovered that the oven was not on the same metered system. By opening the oven door in this small cottage we could luxuriate in warmth without having to keep feeding the meter. There is immense value in spending time in prayer on a regular basis, but that is not about keeping enough prayer in the God-meter for a good day. It is about luxuriating in the warmth of the presence of God.

The great evangelist Dr Billy Graham, at the age of ninety-two in 2010, did an interview on Fox News. In answer to the question of what he would do differently if he had his time again he replied, "I would study more, pray more, travel less, take less speaking engagements." However, in case we immediately hear this as if he were saying he would ask God for more people to have become Christians under his ministry, he goes on, "If I had it to do over again, I'd spend more time in meditation and prayer and telling the Lord how much I love him and adore him and am looking forward to the time we are going to spend together for eternity."

The "are you ready for a miracle" God

In the 1992 movie *Leap of Faith*, Steve Martin plays Jonas Nightengale, a cynical preacher who uses revival meetings to con people out of their money. During one tent meeting, while the gospel choir sings "Are you ready for a miracle", Jonas feels a "healing coming on" and misleads the crowd with showmanship and the clever preparation of his team. The movie plays with issues of faith, disbelief, and evidence of healing, and the surprising event of an unplanned and unexpected miracle which shocks and changes Jonas.

The movie lampoons the revival tent meetings of North America where evangelists wow their audiences with supernatural healings. Typically people are asked to come forward for prayer, at which time the evangelist or his team lay hands upon the person with the result of speaking in tongues, being "slain in the Spirit", or testimony to healing. This is claimed to show that God answers prayer in a miraculous way.

I have never been involved directly in an itinerant tent ministry. But I have participated in evangelistic meetings and conventions on both sides of the Atlantic in which people pray for God to move in miraculous ways – this would be explicit prayer of leaders and preachers before such meetings. While I have never seen blatant exploitation of a crowd for money, I have to say that there have been a number of occasions when I have been uncomfortable in seeing false claims of miracles and a subtle kind of pressure exerted to produce "results". As a young Christian, I heard a preacher say that he had asked God before the sermon to reveal those in the congregation who needed to make a first-time commitment to God. He then pointed directly to me and said, "The Lord tells me that it is you." I looked behind me thinking he was just pointing in my direction but found that I was on the back row! Whatever the Lord wanted to say to me that evening was not in all honesty what the preacher thought he had for me. Then there are the meetings where emotional tricks are used to build up a response from the audience. A leader asks for people to come forward for healing during the singing of a song, and no one comes forward. The preacher invites again and says we will sing the song again, and again and again. I once met someone who did walk forward in such a meeting. I asked what she wanted prayer for, to which she replied, "Oh nothing; I just felt sorry for the preacher!" Now I do believe in prophetic words, healing, and the practice of inviting people to respond to God by coming forward for prayer. But I think that such things have to be done gently, giving space for both response and no response, and in an atmosphere where we acknowledge that we sometimes get things wrong.

The trouble is that in some situations God answering prayer in a miraculous way is completely tied up with the validation of the ministry of the preacher or evangelist. We want the evidence of a miracle to show that our prayer and ministry is powerful, and therefore we are tempted to try to manipulate God or the people to get this.

As *Leap of Faith* cleverly suggests, God is not a God to be manipulated. One of the surprising experiences of the Christian life is when God responds in unusual ways which are not expected or indeed prayed for. Some years ago I found myself preaching at an event in a large US city. The reason I was at this particular event was that a church down the road had invited me from the UK and could not cover all of the travel expenses. So another church, which had not really heard of me, agreed to make use of me and share the expense. It was obvious from the beginning that I was not the main draw. I guess to get people to come along there was free food, musicians, and even clog dancers before I was to speak. As I began to speak at the end of the evening, one of the strongest thunderstorms ever to hit the city began. The large hall where we were was shaking, and the thunderstorm seemed to have been perfectly choreographed with the text of my sermon!

At the end of this evening of fried chicken and clog dancers, there was such a sense of the presence of God I invited people forward to commit their lives afresh to God. So many people flocked forward that after forty minutes the pastor announced we were going to have to end the event, and the people who were still queueing would have to come back the following evening! Of course there are numerous questions here about God working in a storm, which we will come back to later. But for the moment, it is enough to note that no one, especially me, expected or prayed for this kind of evening.

The view that prayer is all about asking God for a miracle is widespread. No longer do you need to have a tent ministry come to your town; you can find all the claims you want on the web and indeed advice on how to pray for these miracles.

"Prayers are a ladder reaching up to heaven. All Prayers are always answered. The Power to work miracles belongs to you," reads one website encouraging the reader to trust in the ministry of the organization running the website. The book *Miracle Prayer* by Dr Susan Shumsky promises nine steps to creating prayers that "get results". David J. Stewart says that "God doesn't expect the impossible from us, He wants us to expect the impossible from Him... Answered prayer can only happen by a miracle of God."[6] Linda Evans Shepherd's *When You Need a Miracle: How to Ask God for the Impossible* claims to teach readers how to reach out to God and ask for a miracle. This book was endorsed by Don Piper, someone

6   http://www.jesus-is-savior.com/Believer%27s%20Corner/miracle_of_
prayer.htm

who claims that he spent "90 minutes in heaven", in the words of his own book, having died for that period of time before being brought back to life. Piper says of the author's claims in *When You Need a Miracle*, "'If you read this book until the end, you will experience miracles' I read it. I did ... God makes the impossible possible every day. Sometimes we just need something to remind us how to ask for it."[7]

Here the language of miracles is very interesting. It uses terms such as "supernatural cause" or "impossible", contrasting God's acts to our normal experience of the world, or even further, breaking the laws of science. The appeal to this kind of miracle is then used as one of the arguments for the existence of God.

We shall of course turn to the concept of miracle and how God might answer prayer within a universe described by the laws of physics in a later chapter. However, it is important to pause here and acknowledge some of the consequences for this kind of view of prayer.

One of the earliest arguments against a God who worked by miracles was summarized by the philosopher Baruch Spinoza in the seventeenth century as the "sheer absurdity"[8] of a God who creates the laws of nature that describe the whole of the universe and then contravenes them simply in response to the prayer of an individual Christian. This was

7 Evans Shepherd, L. (2012). *When You Need a Miracle: How to Ask God for the Impossible*. Grand Rapids, MI: Revell, p. 11.

8 Spinoza, B. (1670). *Tractatus Theologico-Politicus*. London: Trübner and Co., 1862, p. 128.

based on the conviction that the laws of nature reflect God's will, so how can he change his mind so readily and for such trivial reasons? Voltaire in the eighteenth century followed a similar kind of argument, saying it is "impossible a being infinitely wise can have made laws to violate them".[9] In fact, a more recent argument has been put by Christine Overall that miracles would in fact count as evidence against the existence of God. She argues that you cannot have it both ways – if you use evidence of the order and harmony of the universe for the existence of God, then you cannot use the breaking of that order and harmony also as evidence for God. But she also suggests that an all-powerful God, who intervenes in a miraculous way, has to intervene far more often than even the above stories and even Christian tradition claims. If God does not intervene then God is morally defective.[10]

This brings us back to perhaps the central problem of prayer: why does God not answer more prayers, especially in the midst of the suffering of the innocent?

The "pray what you want it doesn't change anything" God

Billy Graham once playfully suggested, "The only time my prayers are never answered is on the golf course." In a more serious mode, the trouble Billy Graham and many other Christians have is the experience of perceiving that God

9   Voltaire (1764). "Philosophical Dictionary". *The Works of Voltaire*, 11. New York: E. R. DuMont, 1901, p. 273.
10 Overall, C. (1985). "Miracles as Evidence Against the Existence of God". *The Southern Journal of Philosophy*, 23, pp. 47–53.

does not seem to answer prayer. The temptation from this experience is to say that prayer may help the person who prays but that is all that it does.

For those who believe in the existence of God, there is an option to believe that everything is determined by God from the moment of creation. After all, God did create everything and so some argue that everything follows his unfolding plan. This view is strengthened by those who want to guard God's grace and power in bringing salvation to the world. This led to some of the theological followers of John Calvin describing a world of double predestination – where some were predestined by God for heaven and some for hell (although it is important to point out that Calvin himself was not as vocal on this as some of his followers). This sense of a God determining everything, and effectively human free will being illusory, does not obviously encourage petitionary prayer – what is the point of praying if everything will already happen anyway? – although a few theologians say that at least you will be sure that your prayers are answered!

I do not find this picture of God inspiring in prayer or indeed reflected in the narrative of the Bible, in which the prayer relationship seems often to be a struggle. For example, in a strange story in Genesis 18 Abraham pleads and argues with God to change his mind on destroying Sodom, and Jesus himself in the Garden of Gethsemane asks whether it is possible for the cup of suffering to be taken away from him (Matthew 26:39). Indeed, Christians throughout the centuries have interpreted Jacob's wrestling with a "man" until daybreak as an image of the experience of prayer (Genesis 32:22–32).

These pictures do not seem to present God as the divine dictator, who does not pay attention to anyone else in following his plan. Dallas Willard wrote, "The idea that everything would happen exactly as it does regardless of whether we pray or not is a specter that haunts the minds of many who sincerely profess belief in God. It makes prayer psychologically impossible, replacing it with dead ritual at best."[11]

Yet this view is not just reflected in those who would see God as the one who determines everything. Prayer that does not change anything, apart from perhaps the person who prays, could be because God is simply not there. This is where voices outside the Christian tradition have created highly influential pictures. Perhaps the most influential, although ironically not as significant within his own field of psychoanalysis, is that of the Austrian Sigmund Freud (1856–1939). Freud was interested in the underlying motives of human behaviour, and so religious practices were an obvious application for his thinking. For Freud, faith arises out of the believer's wish and need to have a protective father figure, for religion "satisfies the human thirst for knowledge; it soothes the fear that men feel of the dangers and vicissitudes of life, when it assures them of a happy ending and offers them comfort in unhappiness".[12] This father figure, who also fulfils the need for instruction and

---

11 Willard, D. (1998). *The Divine Conspiracy*. London: William Collins, p. 268–9
12 Freud, S. (1933). "The Question of a Weltanschauung". *New Introductory Lectures on Psychoanalysis*. Standard Edition, 22, p. 161.

a sense of right and wrong, now leads to the construction of an idea of a deity. For Freud, God was not real but something that we need to deal with our psychological fears and desires. After all, "scientific work is the only road which can lead us to a knowledge of reality outside ourselves".[13] Our idea of such a God is nothing but a construct of our minds – or a delusion, as Richard Dawkins would more recently argue.

Far from the dictator God, this image is of a crippled child crying out to a parent who is not there. Freud saw prayer functioning to assure believers that they have an effect on God's will and sharing in God's power, but for him this was nothing beyond reassuring thoughts.

A great number of objections to Christian faith do have a grain of truth in them. Prayer is of comfort in the difficulties of this life and it does give hope. For some people prayer can also be a route to escapism. But Freud was wrong to see science as the only road to knowledge of reality. We can immediately point out that the very statement "scientific work is the only road which can lead us to a knowledge of reality outside ourselves" cannot be verified by science, so how, in Freud's view, can we know that it is true? More importantly, as we shall see, Christian faith is based on evidence and offers that evidence for support of its truth claims. This leads us to the question of what kind of evidence and whether prayer can be experimentally tested.

---

13 Freud, S. (1927). *The Future of an Illusion*. Standard Edition, 21, p. 31.

The "testable" God

If Freud argued that there is no specific scientific evidence for God, then there have been others who have tried to combat this by using scientific methods to study prayer, especially in its effect on healing. These experiments have proved highly controversial and tend to give an impression of God as a passive subject of a scientific enquiry meekly cooperating with the experiment.

At a very basic level, as we have seen, there is good evidence that the practice of prayer is widespread.[14] There is of course a wide variety of what is meant by prayer, from meditation to petitionary prayer. Dein and Littlewood[15] suggest that an individual's prayer life can be viewed on a spectrum ranging from immature to mature. A progression on the scale is characterized by a change in the perspective of the purpose of prayer. Rather than using prayer as a means of changing the reality of a situation, a more mature individual will use prayer to request assistance in coping with immutable problems and draw closer to God or others. This change in perspective has been shown to be associated with an individual's passage through adolescence. However, this definition of maturity can be interpreted in different ways. "Maturity" which sees prayer as simply changing the individual rather than the situation or

14 Francis, L. and Evans, T. (2001). "The Psychology of Christian Prayer: A Review of Empirical Research", in Francis, L. and Astley, J. (eds). *Psychological Perspectives on Prayer*. Leominster, UK: Gracewing.
15 Dein, S. and Littlewood, R. (2008). "The Psychology of Prayer and the Development of the Prayer Experience Questionnaire". *Mental Health, Religion & Culture* 11.1, pp. 39–52.

the world makes a judgment that the true picture is one where God cannot change the world, rather like I am now more mature because I have grown to the stage where I believe that Teenage Mutant Ninja Turtles do not really live in the sewers of New York.

It is certainly the case that evidence exists that points to the effect of the practice prayer has on an individual being positive in their general health and well-being, although the picture is more complex than simply saying that prayer leads to happiness, calm, and focus. For example, a 2008 study examined the relationship between prayer and psychological health among over 2,000 sixth-form pupils in Northern Ireland.[16] The data shows that more frequent prayer is correlated with lower psychoticism ,that is, a personality pattern typified by aggressiveness and interpersonal hostility. However, it also shows that, in Catholic students, frequent prayer is correlated with higher neuroticism scores, a trait characterized by anxiety, fear, and loneliness. Further, it may not be the prayer itself that is making the positive contribution. The practice of prayer may be helping a person in social support or indeed be a placebo effect.[17]

These studies may be complex, but the real controversy comes in studies which try to see whether the prayer of

16 Francis, L. J., Robbins, M., Lewis, C. A. and Barnes, P. L. (2008). "Prayer and Psychological Health: A Study among Sixth-form Pupils Attending Catholic and Protestant Schools in Northern Ireland". *Mental Health, Religion & Culture* 11.1, pp. 85–92.

17 Breslin, M. J. and Lewis, C. A. (2008). "Theoretical Models of the Nature of Prayer and Health: A Review." *Mental Health, Religion & Culture* 11.1, pp. 9–21.

an individual or community has a positive effect on other people. Francis Galton (1822–1911) was one of the first to explore this area, although his purpose was in part satirical.[18] He collected mortality data on monarchs, missionaries, and clergy – that is, those who were prayed for often in church. He found that they lived no longer than others. Yet, in even this simple study you begin to see the difficulties of interpreting such results. Missionaries frequently went to parts of the world where they were susceptible to a whole array of harsh living conditions and new diseases, so how do you compare like with like? It could also be argued that the somewhat narrow genetic line of monarchs does not make them the best medical test case!

The controversy started in earnest in 1872 when the idea was proposed of a "prayer test". If God really answered prayer, then can it be demonstrated? What if a hospital ward became the focus of sustained prayer for a length of time by a group of believers? If prayer works, then the healing and mortality rates should be far better in that ward than in other equivalent hospitals. This idea sparked a national controversy in the UK as to whether it was scientifically, theologically, or morally right to do such a test.[19] Some argued that prayer should be tested in exactly the same way that we would test a new drug, and others added that as science was given as a gift from God it should be used to explore all of our theological beliefs. Yet

---

18 Galton, F. (1872). "Statistical Inquiries into the Efficacy of Prayer". *The Fortnightly Review*, 1 August.

19 Brush, S. G. (1974). "The Prayer Test". *American Scientist* 62, pp. 561–563.

many Christian leaders opposed the suggestion, arguing that God should not be subjected to such testing.

It was a century later before such research was attempted in earnest. In 1988, Randolph Byrd attempted to see the effect of prayer in the context of coronary care. Nearly 400 patients admitted to San Francisco General Hospital's coronary care unit were randomly assigned either to be prayed for or not.[20] The first names and conditions of those selected to be prayed for were passed on to a small group of evangelical Christians who committed themselves to intercession. Both patients and staff were not informed of who was being prayed for in order to preclude any placebo effect.

The medical question here, of course, is how do you assess whether the prayed for patients did better than the others? Byrd claimed that in six of over twenty outcomes, such as the need for diuretics, antibiotics, and ventilation therapy, the prayed-for patients did better. But in other measures, such as length of hospital stay or mortality, there was no difference. Byrd, however, concluded that there seemed to be an effect, and that "intercessory prayer to the Judeo-Christian God has a beneficial therapeutic effect in patients admitted to a CCU". These are difficult experiments to do, never mind the theological dimensions which we will come to in a moment. One of the main problems is how to deal with all the variables. For example, the Byrd study was criticized on the basis of how did you know whether or not

20 Byrd, R. C. (1988). "Positive Therapeutic Effects of Intercessory Prayer in a Coronary Care Unit Population". *Southern Medical Journal* 81 (7), pp. 826–829.

the "non-prayed for" group in fact were being prayed for by their families and friends?

Other small-scale experiments have been tried on bacteria, plants, and mice as well as on humans. Some claimed to see a positive effect and some did not. Inevitably, those that did not never got the media attention and widespread public attention compared with those that did. Overall the evidence shows no effect, or a potentially small effect, with researchers noting that the most methodologically rigorous studies failed to produce significant findings.[21]

In 2006, a major study funded by the John Templeton Foundation became the largest such study ever done in this area. The Study of the Therapeutic Effects of Intercessory Prayer (STEP) applied a large-scale controlled randomized research model to the question and concluded that there was no significant evidence that prayer was effective in reducing complications following heart surgery.[22] Led by Harvard professor Herbert Benson, it used 1,802 coronary artery bypass surgery patients at six hospitals. It attempted to standardize the style of prayer, asking intercessors to include in their prayers the request "for a successful surgery with a

---

21 Masters, K., Spielmans, G. and Goodson, J. (2006). "Are There Demonstrable Effects of Distant Intercessory Prayer? A Meta-analytic Review". *Annals of Behavioral Medicine* 32 (1), pp. 21–26; Hodge, D. R. (2007). "A Systematic Review of the Empirical Literature on Intercessory Prayer". *Research on Social Work Practice* 17 (2), pp. 174–187.

22 Benson, H., Dusek, J. A., Sherwood, J. B., et al. (2006). "Study of the Therapeutic Effects of Intercessory Prayer (STEP) in Cardiac Bypass Patients: A Multicenter Randomized Trial of Uncertainty and Certainty of Receiving Intercessory Prayer". *American Heart Journal* 151 (4), pp. 934–942.

quick, healthy recovery and no complications".

What can we make of such experiments and results? Social psychologist David Myers filed a notarized prediction of the outcome of the STEP experiment before it began.[23] As a Christian, he suggested four reasons "for predicting that intercessory prayer will not exhibit significant healing power for the cardiac care patients of this experiment". His reasons give not only an understanding of this particular experiment but, more broadly, some very useful insights into how God responds to prayer.

First, he argues that the view of prayer being tested is more akin to magic rather than a biblical understanding of God. This biblical understanding sees God at work as much in the healing ministries of doctors and nurses, not simply in miraculous answer to prayer. Indeed Myers raises a crucial question: would the all-wise, all-knowing, all-loving God of the Bible be uninformed or uncaring apart from our prayers? This is important to consider. John Wesley (1703–91) is widely quoted as saying God does nothing except in answer to prayer, but this quotation is often applied far more widely than Wesley intended. Of course God does many, many things apart from prayer, from the creation of the universe, to taking the initiative in salvation, to the unexpected surprises of grace which bless the Christian life. We need to be careful about seeing our prayer as so important that God is controlled by it. Myers rightly quotes J. I. Packer that prayer "is not an

---

23 http://www.davidmyers.org/Brix?pageID=53

attempt to force God's hand, but a humble acknowledgment of helplessness and dependence".[24]

Second, Myers suggests that such an experimental approach to prayer is doomed to failure. There are just too many variables. For example, as we noted earlier, some of the critique of earlier prayer experiments noted the difficulty of considering other prayer for the patients beyond that of intercessors identified in the experiment. Does God ignore these prayers, or only answer prayers if there are sufficient people, praying the right kind of prayer, with the right kind of faith? Why would God not answer the fervent prayer of the patients and their families without the additional prayers of the recruited intercessors?

Third, there are a number of biblical warnings to "not put the Lord your God to the test" (Deuteronomy 6:16). Indeed this is used by Jesus in responding to one of his temptations. But, some will say, what about Gideon's fleece in the book of Judges? Is this not exactly the same as wanting scientific proof from God in answer to prayer, which God then provides on more than one occasion? In Judges 6, Gideon is told by an angel that God has chosen him to deliver his people from the Midianites. But an encounter with an angel apparently is not enough, and Gideon asks for a series of signs, including laying out a fleece and asking first for the fleece to be wet with dew and the ground dry, and then another night the other way around. In some Christian circles, the judges, including Gideon, are

---

24 Packer, J. I. (1961). *Evangelism and the Sovereignty of God*. Downer's Grove, IL: InterVarsity Press, p. 11.

held up to be heroes of the Christian faith. So, the argument goes, if Gideon did it, then it must be right to ask for God to show his hand in such a test to convince an unbelieving world.

Yet this misses completely the point of the overall narrative of the book of Judges. While some judges, including Gideon, are held up as examples for us (Hebrews 11:32–34), the majority of them demonstrate character flaws, weakness of faith, and leave the people whom they are called to deliver worse off than before they came along. The book of Judges is about the downward spiral into sin so that eventually "everyone did as they saw fit" (Judges 21:25). The only true hero of this book is God. Gideon's fleece test is a demonstration of lack of faith and understanding of God. That God does respond to Gideon's request is a demonstration of God's grace and patience rather than biblical justification of putting God to the test.

Fourth, according to Myers, the evidence of history suggests that the prayers of human beings do not manipulate an infinite God. Supremely, he questions whether the biblical evidence of Jesus asking in the Garden of Gethsemane that the cup of suffering might be avoided can inform our theology of prayer: "Should we pray to God as manipulative adolescents – or as dependent pre-schoolers, whose loving parents, already knowing their children's needs, welcome the intimacy?" As C. S. Lewis once commented, "In Gethsemane the holiest of all petitioners prayed three times that a certain cup might pass from Him. It did not. After that the idea that prayer is recommended to us as a sort of infallible gimmick may be dismissed."[25]

Myers was right in his prediction of a null result – that is, there was no significant improvement in the cardiac care patients being prayed for – and his reasons highlight the theological questions of the kind of God who is imaged in this kind of experiment.

For similar reasons I have always been very sceptical of such experiments. That is not to say that the many different disciplines of science should not be deployed to aid in a better understanding of prayer. Neuroscience might help us in what is actually going on in the brain. Psychology and sociology can help us in understanding how personality, illness, and communities shape the experience of prayer. Indeed, as we shall see in Chapters 4 and 5, physics may give us insights into how God works. But this is a long way from confining God to the experimental laboratory and limiting his degrees of freedom so that certain variables can be tested. If there is a theme that will emerge throughout this book it is that the God encountered in prayer is a free agent rather than at the beck and call of our prayers. But if God is free in such a way, is there any point in trying to understand how he responds to our prayers?

The "it's all mysterious" God

In one of his stand-up routines, the comedian Ricky Gervais bemoans a religious education teacher who cannot give adequate answers to the questions and challenges that the teenage atheist Gervais poses him. The teacher is trying to say that everything happens under God's control, but Gervais challenges this by asking why newborn babies are taken from their parents or why some people are born into abject poverty. No doubt to get himself out of the hole, the teacher responds by saying, "Because God moves in mysterious ways." Gervais wryly comments that this is the theological equivalent of saying "look over there" and then running off in case you are caught!

The phrase is known perhaps most famously in William Cowper's 1774 hymn which has this first verse:

> *God moves in a mysterious way*
> *His wonders to perform;*
> *He plants His footsteps in the sea*
> *And rides upon the storm.*

The story goes that this is the last hymn that Cowper wrote. Struggling with depression and doubt, he takes a cab one night to go to the River Thames with the intention to commit suicide. One version of the story has thick fog coming down, which means that the driver could not find the river, while another version has the driver deliberatively avoiding the river. Eventually, and to Cowper's astonishment, they arrive back at where they started. Cowper interpreted this as God's providential will keeping him safe, and so the following verses:

> *Deep in unfathomable mines*
> *Of never failing skill*
> *He treasures up His bright designs*
> *And works His sovereign will.*
>
> *Ye fearful saints, fresh courage take;*
> *The clouds ye so much dread*
> *Are big with mercy and shall break*
> *In blessings on your head.*

Of course Cowper's story is not primarily about prayer; rather it is about trying to understand what God is doing in suffering and uncertainty. Yet many have used "God moves in mysterious ways" to caution that human beings should not be trying to understand how God works in the world. Isaiah 55:6–9 is also used to support this kind of position:

> *Seek the Lord while he may be found; call on him while*
> *he is near. Let the wicked forsake their ways and the*
> *unrighteous their thoughts. Let them turn to the Lord, and*
> *he will have mercy on them, and to our God, for he will*
> *freely pardon. "For my thoughts are not your thoughts,*
> *neither are your ways my ways," declares the Lord. "As the*
> *heavens are higher than the earth, so are my ways higher*
> *than your ways and my thoughts than your thoughts."*

Is it the case that God is a mystery and therefore the kind of question posed in the title of this book is without hope of an answer or even, perhaps, blasphemous?

Boyer and Hall, in their book *The Mystery of God*, helpfully point out a number of important considerations in addressing such a question. If God really is mysterious in our everyday understanding of the word, then he is indeed completely unknowable and all we can do is confess our ignorance and stay silent. But this then means any talk of or exploration of prayer is ruled out. However, the Bible holds together mystery and revelation. To say that God is a mystery is not to confess our total ignorance; it is to say that the mystery of God has been revealed. Thus it is the God who speaks in Isaiah who says that his thoughts are higher than our thoughts. Here mystery and rational discussion based on God's self-revelation are not opposed but related. This relationship between mystery and knowledge is seen throughout the Bible and Christian history, where one encounters people of faith who know God and try to understand his ways while simultaneously confessing that God is beyond knowledge. The mystery of God is a caution against the hope that rational discussion can understand all of God's ways. Boyer and Hall suggest that, while we have good grounds for expecting that reason will be unable to master God the creator, we also have good grounds for believing that reason should not be abandoned as vain or worthless.

Why should reason be employed in asking the question, "When I pray, how does God answer?" First there is an apologetic reason, engaging with the questions that both those inside and outside of the church want to ask. I am constantly asked about how God answers prayer. Sometimes it is from folk who cannot comprehend how Christian faith and science can be held together with integrity. Sometimes it is from those who have prayed earnestly for a situation and God has not provided the response that they have been praying for. For some this leads to a crisis and sometimes rejection of Christian faith. While there may not be an easy answer I want to take such questions seriously. Second, the attempt to engage with the question and not simply hide behind an appeal to mystery can affect how we pray. Boyer and Hall note one of the problems of the language of mystery is that it is used in so many different ways. Mystery is often used for a puzzle to be solved. God's actions are not such a puzzle to be solved. Now that is not to say that Christian theologians should not be concerned about the struggle to understand God's ways, and to point out truth and falsehood. Indeed I have often sensed that theology's role is to caution us on what not to say. As we have seen in this chapter, popular images of prayer and God have to be challenged by theological thinking. But in addition, Christian faith always goes beyond a mere intellectual description, as Boyer and Hall point out:

> But whatever approach one adopts, the reason Christians want to understand the mystery of God is not merely that they may set the metaphysical record straight, but that they may live and worship well – and life and worship depend on a right relation to a divine person more than on a right analysis of cosmic metaphysics.[26]

---

26 Boyer, S. D. and Hall, C. A. (2012). *The Mystery of God*. Grand Rapids: Baker Academic, p. xvii.

To ask how God answers prayer is not to find a perfect philosophical explanation but to be motivated and energized to pray and act.

Clearing away the myths

Henri Nouwen once suggested that clearing the decks of some of the false gods of popular religion may prepare our hearts for the God of the Bible. I have examined seven popular myths of God created by various teachings or cultural assumptions about prayer. In doing so we have encountered some key questions, from the nature of faith to the relationship of God to the world described by science. We will come to those questions in subsequent chapters. But supremely I suggest that the central issue is how we see God. It is very easy for God to be seen as mechanical and impersonal, as an indulgent and insecure parent, as an unloving and uncaring deity, as a blind dictator, as an absent parent, as an experimental object or as an unknowable mystery.

If this is the central issue then we must turn to the Bible to see what it really does say about God answering prayer, and how through it and in it we see God.

CHAPTER 3

What Does God Actually Do in the Bible?

Asking God to act in specific ways is only a part of the prayers of the Bible and, indeed, Christian experience and practice. Theologian Richard Foster analysed twenty-one different types of prayer[27] and psychologists Spilka and Ladd suggest that there are over thirty forms of prayer.[28] However, when thinking about prayer in contemporary Christian practice, prayers of intercession or petition are, in the words of psychotherapist and theologian J. Harold Ellens, "dominant over all other kinds of prayerful expressions".[29] When we come to the Bible we often impose this thinking onto its pages, and miss its concern with confession, praise and thanksgiving, adoration, and the sheer delight of being in God's presence.

---

27 Foster, R. J. (1992). *Prayer: Finding the Heart's True Home*. San Francisco: Harper.
28 Spilka, B. and Ladd, K. L. (2013). *The Psychology of Prayer*. New York: The Guildford Press.
29 Ellens, J. H. (1977). "Communication Theory and Petitionary Prayers". *Journal of Psychology and Theology*, 5, pp. 48–54.

The other problem we often have in Western culture is our need to extract too quickly from passages of Scripture overarching principles which can be used in teaching or in presenting the faith. There are some great books on prayer that give an overview of how the Old and New Testaments see prayer and indeed encourage prayer. Seeing principles that are common to prayer across centuries and different contexts is very helpful. However, in the broad brush of such an approach, sometimes the detail, complexity, and puzzling questions concerning prayer are lost. My intention in this chapter is to take a few specific passages from the Bible and explore them in detail to see what they might teach about prayer. I choose them for the simple reasons of often hearing sermons preached from them about prayer and finding that over the years of being a Christian they continue to challenge and intrigue me.

Prayer in the midst of the big political situation

The Canadian comedian Stuart Francis once said, "My children are quick to blame other people – they get that from their mother." When things go wrong it is easy to blame other people. It is also easy to blame God, although those of us within the church would never want to say that publicly. The setting of the prayer of Nehemiah in the Old Testament is that things have gone badly wrong. In 587 BC God's chosen people were humiliated. The Temple was destroyed, the successful Davidic monarchy was long gone, and key groups of leaders and people were deported to Babylon. The questions were clear. Was God punishing them? Were the Babylonian gods more powerful? Could God not deliver them even if he wanted to?

Against this backdrop Nehemiah, following the deportation, has risen in civil society to the role of cupbearer to the king. Hearing from his brother and others about how much of a mess Jerusalem is in (Nehemiah 1:1–3), he asks the king whether he can go back to rebuild the walls and city. It is in this context that the writer of the book gives us various pictures of prayer.

First, prayer flows from deep compassion. On hearing the news from Jerusalem Nehemiah weeps and fasts and prays (Nehemiah 1:4). This period of prayer seems to have gone on for four months before he has the courage and the opportunity to ask the king for permission and resources. We get an insight into what this prayer is about in Nehemiah 1:5–11:

> *Then I said:*
>
> *"Lord, the God of heaven, the great and awesome God, who keeps his covenant of love with those who love him and keep his commandments, let your ear be attentive and your eyes open to hear the prayer your servant is praying before you day and night for your servants, the people of Israel. I confess the sins we Israelites, including myself and my father's family, have committed against you. We have acted very wickedly toward you. We have not obeyed the commands, decrees and laws you gave your servant Moses.*
>
> *"Remember the instruction you gave your servant Moses, saying, 'If you are unfaithful, I will scatter you among the nations, but if you return to me and obey my*

commands, then even if your exiled people are at the
farthest horizon, I will gather them from there and bring
them to the place I have chosen as a dwelling for my Name.'

"They are your servants and your people, whom you
redeemed by your great strength and your mighty hand.
Lord, let your ear be attentive to the prayer of this your
servant and to the prayer of your servants who delight in
revering your name. Give your servant success today by
granting him favor in the presence of this man."

Now the simplistic view of prayer would mean that Nehemiah should have asked for a miracle: "O Lord God, please rebuild miraculously the walls of Jerusalem – and do it immediately." In fact, the prayer that is recorded has nothing to do with this. It is a prayer that goes much deeper in exploring the nature of God, and his relationship with Nehemiah and his people. There is in the prayer an acknowledgment of the greatness and awesome nature of God (verse 5) and a remembering of God's power seen in the exodus of delivering his people from Egypt (verse 10). The sense is not first and foremost of "give me a miracle"; it is rather a time of prayer focused on the faithfulness of God whatever the circumstances. This leads to Nehemiah confessing not only his own sins but also the sins of his people.

The obvious message of this passage, often ignored, is that prayer does not always save us from the very worst of circumstances. As Jerusalem was falling and indeed during the many years of exile, one cannot imagine that no one prayed for deliverance. Nehemiah's prayer is a reminder that in such circumstances God does care and he is able to change the situation, but up to this point he has not. The reason for this is not fully explained, but the clear indication is that this is the natural result of political and spiritual choices made by the people.

Nehemiah did not need to engage in this kind of prayer. After all, life for him was pretty good. He was a trusted official on holiday with the king's court in Susa, the winter palace of the Persian kings. Nehemiah is not presented as a priest, or a prophet, or even someone who experiences a dramatic call from God to go back and rebuild Jerusalem. If I am honest I find this immensely challenging. Too often my prayer life centres on what is important to me – my family, friends, and work. It is about making life more comfortable, and a winter palace retreat with the royal family sounds rather attractive. But concern for people in need energizes Nehemiah in prayer.

It is reminiscent of a passage from the New Testament:

> *Jesus went through all the towns and villages, teaching in their synagogues, proclaiming the good news of the kingdom and healing every disease and sickness. When he saw the crowds, he had compassion on them, because they were harassed and helpless, like sheep without a shepherd. Then he said to his disciples, "The harvest is plentiful but the workers are few. Ask the Lord of the harvest, therefore, to send out workers into his harvest field."*
>
> Matthew 9:35–38

It is the word *compassion* that always strikes me when I read this passage. When Jesus saw the crowds he had compassion for them and out of this he encourages his disciples to pray. The word is not a mildly sentimental feeling; it means a stomach-churning experience, something that affects you right to the bottom of your being.

Second, prayer is coupled with action. For four months Nehemiah prays. Then a moment comes when the king asks him why he is sad and then asks, "What is it you want?" (2:4). Here Nehemiah prays what contemporary Christian spirituality has called an "arrow" prayer: "I prayed to the God of heaven and I answered the king" (2:4–5). Nehemiah not only asks to go to Jerusalem but also for letters of safe passage, and resources to rebuild the walls (2:5–9). There is no sense here of prayer asking God to do all the work while he stays in the safety of the royal palace. Indeed in the Matthew passage above it is interesting to note that the answer to the prayer of the disciples to send out more workers into the harvest field is the disciples themselves, as only a few verses later they are sent out by Jesus (Matthew 10:5). They become the answer to their own prayer. When I pray, part of what God does is to change me and involve me more in his work.

Too often prayer has been separated from action. For Nehemiah it was never an either/or. As he rebuilds the walls he is mocked, threatened, and opposed by a number of enemies. His response is, "But we prayed to our God and posted a guard day and night to meet this threat" (Nehemiah 4:9). The chapel of St John's College where I pray regularly is a physical reminder of this. St Mary the Less was originally built as a chapel for the guards who patrolled the walls of Durham city!

This integration of prayer and action is always important to understand. Christian life has opposite temptations. One is a Christian activism which believes we can do everything without prayer and without God. Bishop Stephen Cottrell's book *Hit the Ground Praying* is an important corrective to models of leadership and discipleship which neglect this. But there is another temptation. This is to believe we simply hand everything over to God and leave him to do it all. Often quoted at this point is the life of George Müller (1805–98), an extraordinary Christian leader who cared for orphans in Bristol, the work growing to a complex of buildings for more than 2,000 children. Müller is presented as one of the great models of prayer in that he never asked for money, only prayed for God to provide for the work. This is how Müller lived, but his life was more than just blind faith. Müller was convinced that only as he surrendered his life to the purposes of God and put others before himself would God respond to prayer. Further, reading his journal you see how this was not an easy life. Sometimes the money would not seem to be there until the last possible moment. Müller's confidence in prayer should not be understood as that of a quiet contemplative divorced from the world. His was a rollercoaster life of prayer and action, trust and stress, dependency and leadership.

I sometimes wonder how these insights of compassion

and action are integrated into my own prayer life and the prayer life of my local church. I find the most powerful times of prayer are when the intercessions pick up themes and images from news stories or events in the community which have moved me during the week. I am a very visual person and so projected images on a screen make a huge difference to my prayer – I have never found closing my eyes in prayer to be particularly helpful! I also find myself regularly praying when listening to, watching, or reading on the web the day's news.

The integration of prayer and action is also an area where churches can be very weak. Committee meetings on the use of finances, building or strategy, which begin with prayer and end with people saying the grace together, do little to energize prayer or recognize the bigger perspective of God's kingdom. When I led a church in Liverpool we would pause meetings at crucial moments for time together in open prayer – and those on committees needed to understand that this was part of the responsibility of leadership.

Prayer for a friend in need

Sometimes the teaching of the Bible on prayer is clear and straightforward. Yet sometimes we need to spend more time with the text to grasp the more complex manner of how God responds. Some biblical passages are rather like a good detective story. My favourite detective is Miss Marple. I love the subversion of power as this little old lady solves the crime. It is intriguing and part of the mystery genre when she notices a clue and it is only later in the story when she shows you what has actually happened in a completely different way to our expectations.

Take for example, Mark 2:1–12:

A few days later, when Jesus again entered Capernaum, the people heard that he had come home. They gathered in such large numbers that there was no room left, not even outside the door, and he preached the word to them. Some men came, bringing to him a paralyzed man, carried by four of them. Since they could not get him to Jesus because of the crowd, they made an opening in the roof above Jesus by digging through it and then lowered the mat the man was lying on. When Jesus saw their faith, he said to the paralyzed man, "Son, your sins are forgiven."

Now some teachers of the law were sitting there, thinking to themselves, "Why does this fellow talk like that? He's blaspheming! Who can forgive sins but God alone?"

Immediately Jesus knew in his spirit that this was what they were thinking in their hearts, and he said to them, "Why are you thinking these things? Which is easier: to say to this paralyzed man, 'Your sins are forgiven,' or to say, 'Get up, take your mat and walk'? But I want you to know that the Son of Man has authority on earth to forgive sins." So he said to the man, "I tell you, get up, take your mat and go home." He got up, took his mat and walked out in full view of them all. This amazed everyone and they praised God, saying, "We have never seen anything like this!"

Now some will say that this is a straightforward passage and has been applied to prayer in the following way. In prayer we "bring" our friends to Jesus for healing. If we have enough faith then God will heal.

Yet let us look at a few puzzling clues. The first is in verse 1, "when Jesus again entered Capernaum" a few days later. This should make us remember to look earlier in Mark's Gospel to see when he was previously at Capernaum:

> *They went to Capernaum, and when the Sabbath came, Jesus went into the synagogue and began to teach. The people were amazed at his teaching, because he taught them as one who had authority, not as the teachers of the law. Just then a man in their synagogue who was possessed by an impure spirit cried out, "What do you want with us, Jesus of Nazareth? Have you come to destroy us? I know who you are – the Holy One of God!"*
>
> *"Be quiet!" said Jesus sternly. "Come out of him!" The impure spirit shook the man violently and came out of him with a shriek.*
>
> *The people were all so amazed that they asked each other, "What is this? A new teaching – and with authority! He even gives orders to impure spirits and they obey him." News about him spread quickly over the whole region of Galilee.*
>
> *As soon as they left the synagogue, they went with James and John to the home of Simon and Andrew. Simon's mother-in-law was in bed with a fever, and they immediately told Jesus about her. So he went to her, took her*

hand and helped her up. The fever left her and she began to wait on them.

That evening after sunset the people brought to Jesus all the sick and demon-possessed. The whole town gathered at the door, and Jesus healed many who had various diseases. He also drove out many demons, but he would not let the demons speak because they knew who he was.

Mark 1:21–34

Jesus had been in Capernaum before and indeed exercised a powerful ministry. Exorcisms and healings caused a huge stir, and Mark tells us that the people brought "all the sick and demon-possessed" to Jesus. Yet note that he did not heal all of them but "many". So we can infer that the paralysed man of Mark 2 was one of those who was not healed when Jesus was in Capernaum previously. We know little about him, not even his name. But we can speculate that he was somewhat frustrated! With so many people healed, why was he left out? Being paralysed in the ancient world meant that he was a huge burden on family and friends and also there would have been many times when well-meaning friends must have suggested it was his own fault or sin that had caused it, just as the friends of Job had done. No reason is given as to why he was not one of the people healed the first time.

However, he had some good friends. They too must have been asking why he had not been healed before, but hearing that Jesus was back they wanted to make sure this time. Yet they discovered that others had "gathered in such large numbers that there was no room left, not even outside the door" (2:2). You can imagine their frustration, thinking *not again*! Houses that have been excavated in Capernaum show small rooms, seldom reaching to as much as 5 metres, with the width limited by the length of tree trunks available for roofing. People were everywhere, packed into the house and packed around it. Now, as one commentator wryly observes, if they had been women they would probably have negotiated their way through the situation, but being angry men they could only think of violent action! The house would have been single storey with a flat roof, accessible by an outside staircase and used for working and sleeping, so it was not too flimsy. The men literally "unroofed the roof", a major demolition job, by "digging it out". One has great sympathy with the owner of the house! It is an interesting picture of "faith".

Then comes the second puzzling clue in this story. Lowered down in the midst of this major deconstruction of the roof, among all the embarrassment and uncertainty of what was going to happen, the man hears Jesus say, "Son, your sins are forgiven" (Mark 2:5). At this I can't help but feel sorry for the man! I can imagine him looking at Jesus and saying, "Come on Jesus. That's not what I've come for. I've had plenty of people say 'cheer up son; it will never happen', 'every cloud has a silver lining', 'trials are sent to test us', and other such comforting things. And by the way, how many sins do you think I've been able to commit if I have to be carried everywhere?" Or at least words to that effect. And what must his friends have been thinking after going to all this trouble?

Why does Jesus say "your sins are forgiven" when it is obvious that the man wants to walk? While the Bible does link together sin and illness in general terms – after all, we are part of a fallen world – Jesus never endorses that physical illness is the direct result of an individual's sin. In John 9:2–3, when asked whether it is the man or his parents who had sinned to cause the man's blindness, Jesus explicitly says neither. In this case, Jesus' response to the faith of the friends bringing the paralysed man has a much deeper dimension. It is a point which the religious teachers immediately pick up on. They think to themselves that this is blasphemy, for "Who can forgive sins but God alone?" Jesus is making the claim that he is God. This exchange will be part of a major narrative thread throughout Mark's Gospel – that of the tension between Jesus and the religious teachers. When he was in Capernaum before, "he taught them as one who had authority, not as the teachers of the law" (1:22), and this threat to their position leads them eventually to accuse him of blasphemy and of being in league with the devil (3:22). This incident is part of a bigger narrative of who Jesus is, rather than just the needs of one individual.

It is difficult in prayer sometimes to remember this very simple point. In the frustration of personal need, and in the hope of release, we judge God's responses to our prayer in a very isolated way, not allowing the possibility of some bigger story at work. Sometimes that bigger story is not at all clear to us. Well-meaning Christians sometimes feel the need to try to explain fully the story with clichés or half-formed theology.

I once met a man who rejected the existence of God when a pastor told him that the death of his sister in childhood was because God wanted another "star in heaven". Even as a child the man knew that stars in fact came from collapsing gas clouds in the galaxy, but more importantly he felt guilty that his sister might not have died if he had stopped her from running out into the road.

Jesus explodes the carefully constructed view of God and life that the religious teachers built up. Mark is telling us as readers of the story the same message. This Jesus explodes our carefully constructed and sometimes overly simplistic view of the world. Indeed, when it comes to prayer, I find the accounts of Jesus challenging and inspiring in equal measure. They are a constant caution that my view of God and the world is indeed very small.

Perceiving the kind of thoughts at work in the religious teachers, Jesus challenges them even more directly by showing them that he has the authority to forgive sins by enabling the man to walk. No wonder the people say they have never seen anything like this!

The story is about a miracle, but it gives us clues that how God responds to our requests has deeper dimensions. Not everyone is healed, Jesus works in unexpected ways, and the individual's needs are not always the only thing in play in God's interaction with the world. And faith can take a number of forms. In the friends of the paralysed man there is no articulation of Jesus as the Son of God or Lord, no articulation of the belief that he can heal their friend – just a complex mess of frustration, desire, violent action, and some perhaps even superstitious hope that if they get their friend in front of Jesus then there is a chance that things might be different.

It is a reminder to me of the human complexity of prayer. There have been many times that I have prayed with motives stemming from selfishness rather than compassion for others. Of course there are many mixed motives in human action, and this is true of prayer also. Both my parents had difficult times in hospital at the end of their lives. It was clear that they would not recover, so I found myself struggling with what to pray for. There was part of me that wanted to pray for a quick and peaceful death so that they would be freed from the suffering. But I could not deny that part of that prayer was selfish. This was because of the weariness of constant visiting, the emotional toil of seeing them suffer, and all of the other areas of life that I had to maintain.

If we do trust that God sees and responds to the bigger story, then we can bring all our requests with all their motives to him. I am relaxed enough not to worry about why I am asking, and confident enough that it is sufficient to bring all my concerns into his presence.

Praying with faith

On a website which commends "the prayer of faith" as "prayer that gets results", the author notes that when he prays the Lord always answers. This prayer of faith is asking for, believing in, and receiving a particular outcome.[30] Faith, he argues, does not allow any doubt of any kind at any time. When I was a young Christian I preached a sermon on the way that the questions that Thomas asks of Jesus in John's Gospel lead him into a deeper knowledge of Jesus. After I finished a woman approached me and began, "Now then young man..." That is never a promising beginning to a conversation after a sermon! "You seemed to suggest," she went on, "that you have had doubts in your faith." "Yes," I replied, and before I could get out what I meant by that she cut in, "Well, if you had faith, you would have no doubts at all."

At first glance, there does seem to be biblical support for the view that effective prayer is wholly dependent on faith: "Therefore I tell you, whatever you ask for in prayer, believe that you have received it, and it will be yours" (Mark 11:24).

The following passage also suggests that prayers offered in faith will be answered:

> Is anyone among you in trouble? Let them pray. Is anyone happy? Let them sing songs of praise. Is anyone among you sick? Let them call the elders of the church to pray over them and anoint them with oil in the name of the Lord. And the prayer offered in faith will make the sick person well; the Lord will raise them up. If they have sinned, they will be forgiven. (James 5:13–15)

What does it mean to pray with faith? Is it rather like that scene in *Peter Pan*, when Captain Hook has poisoned Tinker

---

30 http://www.biblecities.com/prayer-of-faith.htm

Bell? Tinker Bell's light is fading, and the audience is told, "She's going to die unless we do something. Clap your hands! Clap your hands and say, 'I believe in fairies!'" Is faith the way we work ourselves up to really believe? Or is faith a bit like an access all areas pass at a rock concert, getting you into the inner sanctum of God?

Many people both outside and inside the Christian tradition find this difficult. If only we have enough faith then God will answer our prayer; the fact that God does not seem to answer then questions the reality of faith. In fact, a number of Christians feel guilty for not having enough faith in the face of illness and death of loved ones. Have we let doubt creep in and is it our fault? Did we not clap our hands loud enough and say "I believe in God" with enough conviction?

But what actually is faith in this context? Is it simply convincing ourselves that what we are praying for is going to happen? I remember the confidence of the coach of our junior football team who said that all we had to do was believe that we were going to win this game, before we were beaten 22-0. The power of positive thinking does not always give positive results.

Faith is a complex word in the Bible having many nuances in its meaning, but at its heart it is very simple. Faith is not a quantity or a quality; rather it is a relational commitment to God. As the great missionary to China Hudson Taylor (1832–1905) rightly observed, "The issue is not greater faith, but faith in a great God." If God is therefore the central focus of praying with faith, then a number of things follow.

First, there is no one pattern of faith to be copied or steps to be followed in order to make faith. Faith is not produced by some kind of bargain with God. In the classic *Simpsons* episode where a hurricane hits Springfield, Marge Simpson, sheltering from the hurricane with a fearful family, prays, "If you stop this hurricane and save our family we will be forever grateful and recommend you to all our friends." When the hurricane stops, Homer remarks, "He fell for it!"

The disciples once raised the question of faith with Jesus: "The apostles said to the Lord, 'Increase our faith!' He replied, 'If you have faith as small as a mustard seed, you can say to this mulberry tree, "Be uprooted and planted in the sea," and it will obey you'" (Luke 17:5–6). The trouble is that when we read this we start thinking about quantity of faith. My faith is more like a grain of sand rather than a mustard seed, and only if I had more, then I would be able to have prayers answered. But we are missing, with our usual Western obsession to quantify, the whole point of the passage. Pete Grieg, one of the founders of the international movement 24-7 Prayer, says that Jesus is saying that size doesn't matter – small as a mustard seed or grain of sand is fine because what really matters is the powerful God of love.

It is certainly the case that in many but not all of Jesus' healing miracles he points to the faith of those who come to him. But that faith is diverse in the extreme. Sometimes it is represented by taking the roof off a house. Sometimes it is represented by a woman coming up and touching the cloak of Jesus and hoping to get away without being spotted (Matthew 9:21–23). Sometimes it is shown in someone who clearly expresses the belief that Jesus can heal at a distance (Luke 7:1–10), and sometimes it is the answer of a blind man to Jesus' question of what he wants (Mark 10:51–52). What is common to all is that they simply came to Jesus, with mixed motives, mixed beliefs, and indeed mixed actions. But they were responding to and placing their trust in him.

Second, faith recognizes the centrality of the will of God in prayer. At one level knowing the will of God is very easy. God has revealed his will in the pages of Scripture and we are asked to live our lives in conforming to it. He promises to give us the confidence of praying for things in God's will. So when we pray for the power of the Holy Spirit to come into our lives we can have confidence in praying because God has promised to pour out the Holy Spirit. This is not the same attitude as that of the "health and wealth" contract type of prayer we saw in the last chapter, nor is it the attitude that says I can earn answered prayer by living perfectly. It is simply recognizing that I put God at the centre.

In fact, as a young Christian I would agonize over the will of God, trying to work out whether God wanted me to make this or that particular decision – about a relationship or a career path. Then I began to realize that I already knew 99.9999 per cent of what God wanted me to do with my life as it had been revealed in Scripture – to love God and to love neighbour in following Jesus. As I began to try to respond to that the specific decisions seemed to become more natural.

However, when it comes to prayer for specific things, especially for the healing of individuals, then this sense of faith and the will of God becomes more complex. For some at particular times, a special assurance or inner conviction of something to pray for seems to be given. It is interesting that in the passage from James above, the writer goes on to link this instruction with the example of Elijah: "Elijah was a man just like us. He prayed earnestly that it would not rain, and it did not rain on the land for three and a half years" (James 5:17).

But it is clear from the story in 1 Kings 17–18 that Elijah had received a sense of God's will in the matter. I have sometimes been involved in prayer ministry where someone has been given a sense from God that healing will happen. I don't understand how or why this happens but it does. Equally, I have been involved in prayer ministry where either the sick person or one of the people praying expresses that they have received a word from God, but there is no healing. Sometimes we simply get it wrong, it seems.

Maturity in prayer means learning to live with some of these unanswered questions. It remains open to God being involved in a number of different ways, recognizes our weakness as human beings to read God's will, and accepts the times when God does not heal.

One of my great heroes in the Christian faith is the Anglican church leader and evangelist David Watson. At the height of his ministry he contracted cancer. Prayer was said for him throughout the world. John Wimber, pioneer of "power evangelism", which brought belief in signs and wonders even more to the forefront of charismatic renewal, came from California to pray for his friend and anoint him with oil. But there came a time when both men accepted that no assurance had been given of a healing and therefore it was time to recognize that it no longer made sense to keep praying for miraculous healing.

The mistake in interpretation of the James passage above is to think that somehow the "prayer of faith" can be learnt from others, or that it can be created by drawing a long breath, shutting your eyes, and "believing as many as six impossible things before breakfast". It is a gift which is given on rare occasions, and not just to the great prophets and priests.

Then how do we pray with faith in situations where such a gift is not given? Do we simply not pray at all? Here we need to remember that faith is about our relationship with God – and that relationship is created, sustained, and redeemed by God's generosity. Faith is our response to God's initiative of love, a placing of trust in God. Faith recognizes the primacy of the will and knowledge of God in all things. Some will say that to preface prayer with "Lord, if it be your will…" undermines faith and exposes doubt. I think it is exactly the opposite because it puts God at the focus of prayer rather than our desires and limited knowledge of the situation.

We get an example of this in Mark 1:40–42:

> *A man with leprosy came to him and begged him on his
> knees, "If you are willing, you can make me clean." Jesus
> was indignant. He reached out his hand and touched the
> man. "I am willing," he said. "Be clean!" Immediately the
> leprosy left him and he was cleansed.*

The man does know and believe that Jesus can heal him but he submits to Jesus' will. Jesus responds (some manuscripts say "full of compassion" rather than "indignant") and heals him. This is the right approach when there is not a clear promise of the Bible or a clear sense of assurance.

However, "Lord, if it be your will..." can be used as a quick get-out clause to avoid the long struggle in prayer which we saw was characteristic of Nehemiah. We need to stay open and to wrestle with the will of God. Part of intercessory prayer is listening as well as asking. It may be that in our eagerness to ask God we do not give time to listen to his will. That is why a time of listening and of waiting on God in silence should be part of prayer. But at times, it is only by blurting our prayer requests out that we get to a point where we can listen.

As a pastor, I learnt very early that when certain people came for advice, I had to give them time to get out their whole story and concerns. It was useless trying to interrupt to pick up, affirm, or challenge specific points. It was like a door had been opened and a flood rather than stream of consciousness was flowing out. If you tried to battle against this flood you were going to lose. You had to wait (sometimes a very long time!) until it was all out and then you could attempt to say something that would be heard. I wonder if prayer is sometimes like that. We have to get all our emotional requests out before we begin to hear God. Indeed it is sometimes in the experience of unanswered prayer that faith is deepened.

When prayer returns unanswered

One of the most difficult spiritual experiences is when prayer is not answered. To ask for anything in any relationship and then to be seemingly rejected or ignored is a crushing experience. When that request is about something which has high importance in our life, the experience can lead to bitterness, a refusal to ask any more, and even to the ending of a relationship. I have met a number of people over the years for whom the experience of unanswered prayer has been the cause for doubting the existence of God.

A discussion thread on Yahoo Answers is titled "Is Prayer Stupid or Not?"[31] It came out of the experience of someone whose father died in hospital despite people praying about the situation. The responses show a number of different attitudes:

- "The primary purpose of prayer is to provide emotional comfort for those engaging in prayer. Prayer has no effect on reality."

- "My belief is that prayer is just talking to yourself."

- "The ways of man and God are not the same."

31 https://answers.yahoo.com/question/index;_
ylt=A9mSs3ebqsVTb30A6J6A3YlQ;_ylu=X3oDMTE0YWNkbTFrBHN
lYwNzcgRwb3MDMTIEY29sbwNpcjIEdnRpZANUQVVLMDFfMQ--
?qid=20100412100421AAxHa98

- "There are such things as unanswered prayers, though. Just because you ask for something doesn't mean you'll get it."

- "Miracles don't happen unless you ask for them... people who pray have a higher rate of receiving a miracle than those who don't."

This common reaction is to try to explain why prayers are unanswered. Yet the Bible itself has a number of instances of unanswered prayer or situations where the action of Jesus is somewhat perplexing. Often no explanation is given.

In John 11 there is a story of sickness, doubt, and death for those whom Jesus loves. When the name of Lazarus is mentioned, our minds go immediately to his raising at the end of the story but this should not minimize some of the difficult questions earlier in the story.

Lazarus, the brother of Mary and Martha, is sick and the family who seem to be close friends with Jesus send word to him, saying, "Lord, the one you love is sick" (verse 3). It is quite a natural reaction, for already in John's Gospel we have seen the power of God in Jesus, from turning water into wine to restoring sight to the blind. We do not know whether this was the first thing they did, whether it was an immediate emotional response, or whether it was in total desperation. But Jesus decides to stay where he is for two more days. John records Jesus' love for Lazarus and the sisters and that Jesus knows that Lazarus has died, but no clear reason is given as to why Jesus does not respond immediately.

Eventually Jesus decides to go and is met by each of the sisters in turn. The experience of asking Jesus for help and then him not intervening before the death of their brother must have been painful. If he could not have come, then could he not have healed at a distance? Did he really love them? Both greet him with, "Lord, if you had been here, my brother would not have died" (verses 21, 32). You can read this in a number of ways. Was it an expression of continuing trust in Jesus, or was it actually a sense of bitter accusation? Martha does express trust by going on to say, "But I know that even now God will give you whatever you ask" (verse 22) and that she believes in Jesus (verse 27). This is a bold response especially as Lazarus has been dead for four days. Mary simply wept at his feet.

John then records, "When Jesus saw her weeping, and the Jews who had come along with her also weeping, he was deeply moved in spirit and troubled" (verse 33). This doesn't quite fit with the Jesus who earlier in the story seemed to know all that was going on. Now of course, John's understanding of Jesus does not allow us to interpret this as confusion on the part of Jesus, but it does show how the Word who became flesh takes seriously our anger, sadness, and confusion – and is emotionally moved by it. This is a very different picture of God than that of a detached dictator or mechanical slot machine.

Lazarus is restored to life, although one has some sympathy for him. He is going to have to die again at some point, and indeed because of this miracle he becomes the target of the chief priests' plot to kill him (John 12:10–11)!

Nevertheless, this story is important because Mary and Martha exhibit that faith is not trusting in what you want Jesus to do, but trusting in Jesus in the midst of unanswered requests.

A similar experience seems to have been part of the life of the apostle Paul:

> *Therefore, in order to keep me from becoming conceited,*
> *I was given a thorn in my flesh, a messenger of Satan, to*
> *torment me. Three times I pleaded with the Lord to take*
> *it away from me. But he said to me, "My grace is sufficient*
> *for you, for my power is made perfect in weakness."*
> *Therefore I will boast all the more gladly about my*
> *weaknesses, so that Christ's power may rest on me. That*
> *is why, for Christ's sake, I delight in weaknesses, in insults,*
> *in hardships, in persecutions, in difficulties. For when I am*
> *weak, then I am strong.*
>
> 2 Corinthians 12:7–10

The context of the letter of 2 Corinthians is that Paul is having to defend himself against criticism of his life and ministry, not least in contrast to those whom he calls the "super-apostles" – teachers who were beginning to be very influential in the church that Paul had given so much to. From Paul's response in this letter we gather that the criticism is severe: he can't make his mind up (1:17); he is proud and boastful (3:1); he does not have a successful preaching ministry (4:3); he is a questionable apostle (11:5); and he is not eloquent in speaking (11:6). Perhaps most of all, some point to his physical weakness (10:10). Surely this is a sign of lack of faith?

How could the power of the Holy Spirit be at work in him if he is not well? In the phrase of one commentator, they poked fun at him for being "a sick charismatic".

It is remarkable that under such an onslaught Paul is open and transparent about his experience. He speaks about his "thorn in the flesh". Some have argued that this is some kind of spiritual weakness, but most commentators agree that it is most probably a physical affliction. Paul intercedes for this to be removed on three occasions. But here his faith is expressed in his trust that God is at work even if his prayer for the thorn to be removed is not answered. There is honesty here about unanswered prayer which is important and refreshing. Under attack and criticism it would have been easy to try to explain this away. However, Paul sees God at work in this experience of not receiving the answer that he prayed for.

One further and puzzling example comes from the Old Testament, in the life of David, the greatest of Israel's kings and a man after God's own heart. After committing adultery with Bathsheba and having her husband Uriah the Hittite killed, David is confronted by the prophet Nathan who exposes David to his sin through the telling of a parable. The story continues:

> *Then David said to Nathan, "I have sinned against the Lord."*
> *Nathan replied, "The Lord has taken away your sin. You are*
> *not going to die. But because by doing this you have shown*
> *utter contempt for the Lord, the son born to you will die."*
>
> *After Nathan had gone home, the Lord struck the child*
> *that Uriah's wife had borne to David, and he became ill.*

David pleaded with God for the child. He fasted and spent the nights lying in sackcloth on the ground. The elders of his household stood beside him to get him up from the ground, but he refused, and he would not eat any food with them.

On the seventh day the child died. David's attendants were afraid to tell him that the child was dead, for they thought, "While the child was still living, he wouldn't listen to us when we spoke to him. How can we now tell him the child is dead? He may do something desperate."

David noticed that his attendants were whispering among themselves, and he realized the child was dead. "Is the child dead?" he asked.

"Yes," they replied, "he is dead."

Then David got up from the ground. After he had washed, put on lotions and changed his clothes, he went into the house of the Lord and worshiped. Then he went to his own house, and at his request they served him food, and he ate.

His attendants asked him, "Why are you acting this way? While the child was alive, you fasted and wept, but now that the child is dead, you get up and eat!"

He answered, "While the child was still alive, I fasted and wept. I thought, 'Who knows? The Lord may be gracious to me and let the child live.' But now that he is dead, why should I go on fasting? Can I bring him back again? I will go to him, but he will not return to me."

2 Samuel 12:13–23

There is much here which is troubling and really difficult to understand, not least on why the judgment of David's sin is interpreted as the illness and death of an innocent child. Even concerted prayer by David, whose life has been so close to God, cannot make any difference to the situation.

We need to be careful with these kinds of stories. We need to acknowledge the difficulties they pose and understand that they act as a corrective in showing that a too simplistic answer to how God may answer prayer just does not fit with the range of biblical material. There is often simply no easy way to understand or explain away unanswered prayer. Perhaps more honesty among church leaders publicly acknowledging unanswered prayer alongside the "eye-catching" stories of miracles would be helpful.

A major part of the psalms laments the reality of unjust suffering, hopeless circumstances, and indeed unanswered prayers. A psalm attributed to David, while committing to praise God, nevertheless is honest:

> *Yet when they were ill, I put on sackcloth*
> *and humbled myself with fasting.*
> *When my prayers returned to me unanswered,*
> *I went about mourning*
> *as though for my friend or brother.*
> *I bowed my head in grief*
> *as though weeping for my mother.*
>
> Psalm 35:13–14

I have found in my own experience of unanswered prayer that the most transforming moments have been as I have lamented and even expressed anger towards God in worship.

Indeed, they have been a kind of cathartic experience which in its own mysterious way becomes an unexpected positive outcome to prayer.

Prayer where God has freedom to respond

In the context of personal relationships, the person who is asked for something has a number of options. We learn this very well in the parent–child relationship. When my daughter asked to go to a rock concert and some financial help to do it (that is, in the days when I was actually asked), of course I could say, "yes", "no" or "not yet". I remember from my own childhood how frustrating it was when a parent gave an answer that I did not want or indeed understand. There can be, and often is, argument and hurt – but as a parent I want to grow in relationship with my child and I want her not to go off and never speak to me again. In a relationship built upon faith, with love at its heart, we can learn and move on.

It is amazing how easy it is to forget that God may say "yes", "no", "not yet" or indeed something else. Perhaps the way that we have imaged God in the popular myths of Chapter 2 allows us to fall into this trap.

The biblical material on how God answers prayer is not straightforward. It does not give a simple model and say this is how you do it in order to get this answer. God is not a mathematical equation. Indeed, there are parts of the biblical account where we would like to have much more detail, but some of God's ways do remain hidden.

However, all of the biblical material seems united in one thing – that God has the power to do whatever he likes even if he chooses not to do certain things.

It is here that modern science comes into the conversation and questions whether in fact God has the freedom to do anything at all in the universe. It is to this that we turn next.

CHAPTER 4

Out of Date Science and the Problems with Miracles

C harles Darwin (1809–82) wrote in his *Autobiography*, "The more we know of the fixed laws of nature the more incredible do miracles become."[32] It is much debated as to where Darwin was with regard to Christian faith. His wife Emma had a strong Christian faith, and Darwin himself limited some of his own views in respect to his wife. He did start off influenced by the design argument of William Paley (1743–1805), in which Paley suggested that if you wander across a field and find a watch, then from its design you can infer that it has a designer. Paley then used this as an analogy with nature, saying that as you observe the biological world you can see design from

32 Barlow, N. ed. (1958). *The autobiography of Charles Darwin 1809–1882. With the original omissions restored. Edited and with appendix and notes by his granddaughter Nora Barlow*. London: Collins, p. 86.

which you can infer a designer. In fact, Darwin signed up to his voyage on HMS *Beagle* to help the captain of the vessel pursue his interest in the design argument. It was during that voyage that Darwin began to think about natural selection by descent as species adapted to different environments. This explanation of the origin of species became a much stronger explanation for design in the natural world than that of a supernatural creator.

However, the story of Darwin's theological thinking is more complicated than is often recounted. It is clear that Darwin was aware of some of the biblical work done in the nineteenth century by commentators who were critical of the historicity of some of the stories in the Bible. Then, while in Chile, he experienced a massive earthquake and saw the loss of life caused by it. He asked how a designer God could allow this to happen. But most importantly, Darwin's belief in the God of Christian theism never recovered from the death of his beloved child Annie in 1851 at the age of ten. Darwin had a special relationship with her and when she became sick he took her to Malvern for treatment, but there she died. Darwin struggled to understand why a good God could let her die by not answering the fervent prayer of her parents.

These different experiences and insights fed off each other and it seems Darwin moved first to deism, believing that God set up the laws of the universe but did not have the capacity to do anything by way of miracle or special intervention. This view "defended" God against the charge about why he did not do anything to heal illness in the world. Science after all was explaining more and more of the universe, and there seemed to be no room for God to do anything anyway. But of course, this deistic view of God was not created by nineteenth-century science. It was implicit in the very argument to try to prove the existence of God – that of Paley's divine watchmaker. To put it simply, if you buy a watch from a very good watchmaker you do not want to keep asking the watchmaker to correct it every day as it goes wrong. A divine watchmaker would have made a perfect world and therefore has no need to intervene in it; and so there is no need to ask God for anything – there is no need to pray.

While many people will follow Darwin's view that science rules out miracles, it is interesting that in the late twentieth and early twenty-first centuries, there has been a resurgence of interest in miraculous acts in response to prayer. Within the church, the beginning of the Pentecostal movement in the early part of the twentieth century and its amazing growth throughout the world, and the rise of the charismatic movement of the last forty years, has raised the profile of the "supernatural" in many churches, and particularly raised questions about healing. John Wimber's "power evangelism" argues that the Western church has lost spiritual power because of the dominance of a view that "we live in a universe which is closed off from divine intervention, in which truth is arrived at through empirical means and rational thought".[33] In the 1990s,

33 Wimber J. with Springer, K. (1985). *Power Evangelism*. London: Hodder and Stoughton, p. 77.

the movement of the Spirit commonly known as the "Toronto blessing" again raised the question of the supernatural in both the Christian and secular media.

In the light of this we need to examine the way miracles are perceived and how science has been used to argue against their possibility.

The miraculous in the Bible?

It is undeniable that at first reading the Bible is a book which unashamedly records events that are by any definition miraculous. Furthermore, the miracles are an intrinsic part of the story. Jesus turns water into wine at a wedding. John, as he records this act of Jesus, suggests that there is a certain extravagance about it, for it seems Jesus produced between 120 and 180 gallons of wine at a party where most of the guests had already had their fill (John 2:1–10). Elsewhere, Jesus apparently defies gravity and walks on water (Mark 6), feeds 5,000 men plus unnumbered women and children on five loaves and two fish (Mark 6:30–44), and heals those who are sick (Mark 6:56). Even these acts seem almost insignificant alongside the virgin birth and the resurrection.

It is worth noting at this point that there is within the Bible a wide spectrum of cases which are commonly called miracles. Some are clearly not at odds with our known scientific laws. Finding a coin in the mouth of a fish is highly improbable in the statistical sense, but it does not contravene a known law (Matthew 17:27). They could be rare but natural events. However, others – such as water into wine, and the resurrection – do seem to go against our current understanding of the regularities in the universe.

The biblical writers record these stories in a natural and at times almost matter of fact kind of way. It is not enough to immediately dismiss this "matter of fact" way on the basis that the biblical writers did not know modern scientific laws and therefore saw no problem. It might be the case that Peter had no understanding of Newton's law of gravitation or Archimedes' principle, but as a fisherman on the Sea of Galilee he knew it was unusual for people to go for a stroll on the surface of the water!

The writers show little interest, however, in how these things happen. One of the few exceptions is the parting of the Red Sea, which delivers the people of Israel from the pursuing Egyptian chariots. This is understood to be due to a strong east wind (Exodus 14:21). It reminds us that we must be careful not to draw too big a distinction between what we commonly call the "miraculous" and other events. What is important is their meaning or significance.

John's Gospel, of all the parts of the Bible, emphasizes this aspect. John calls the miracles "signs", and they are intricately woven into the story and structure of the Gospel. The signs are coupled together often with the great "I am" statements. Thus, the feeding of the 5,000 is the sign of Jesus' statement, "I am the bread of life." It points towards and embodies Jesus' claim.

Miracles were acknowledged by the early church to be

central to the ministry of Jesus. In the first sermon on the day of Pentecost, Peter says, "Fellow Israelites, listen to this: Jesus of Nazareth was a man accredited by God to you by miracles, wonders and signs, which God did among you through him, as you yourselves know" (Acts 2:22).

It is clear that they were integral as part of the story, not novelties to show how clever God was. But what role did they play? It is difficult to give a short answer to that question. The purpose of miracles across the whole biblical literature is a little more diverse. For example, various answers are given in the New Testament, many of which we have already touched on in the previous chapter:

- The raising from the dead of Lazarus was "for God's glory" (John 11:4).

- It was also a demonstration of the compassion of Jesus (John 11:33, 35, 38).

- They are a demonstration of Jesus as the Son of God (John 20:30–31).

- The healing of the blind man is an acted parable of the way that Jesus will soon open the spiritual eyes of the disciples (Mark 8:22–26).

- Other miracles seem to reveal things about Jesus and the Father, such as the right to forgive sins (Mark 2:1–12).

The common theme is that these actions are more than just acts of mercy, or pointers to the divine origin of Jesus, or to attract the crowds. They are first and foremost signs and indications of the fact that the messianic age has arrived in Jesus. That is, they are a dramatic demonstration of God's reign, or the arrival and character of the kingdom of God through Jesus.

There is a strong tradition in the history of the church of appealing to miracles as recorded in the Scriptures as the foundation of religion. For example, Samuel Clarke, in his 1705 Boyle Lectures, argued that Christianity was proved by signs and miracles, and in 1736 Joseph Butler noted that miracles are one of the "direct and fundamental proofs" of Christianity.[34] It is the same argument that exists today, in the way that some Christians will say "come and see people healed at this meeting and this will prove to you the existence of God". Yet in the New Testament itself, miracles do not lead to proof. Mark records an incident when Jesus was with the disciples in a boat (Mark 8:13–21). The disciples are troubled that they have only one loaf of bread. One can almost hear the frustration in Jesus' voice as he asks them how many basketfuls they collected up after feeding 5,000 with five loaves, and how many basketfuls when 4,000 were fed from seven loaves, events which according to Mark had happened previously (Mark 6:30–44; 8:1–13). Jesus is telling them to do the mathematics! Twelve loaves with Jesus feed 9,000, and that figure leaves out the women and children! Now, work out how many are in the boat, and as long as there are no more than 750 then we'll be all right with one loaf! "Do you still not understand?" says Jesus.

---

34 Butler, J. (1736). *The Analogy of Religion*. Hartford: Samuel G. Goodrich, 1819, p. 173.

The miracles by themselves are not enough for the disciples.

Miracles are not proof but clear pointers which people can recognize if they are open to Jesus. For example, the evidence for the resurrection cannot prove the truth of Christianity. It may be a pointer that there is more to this universe than meets the eye, that Jesus is really who he said he was, and that death is not the end. Confirmation of the evidence comes with experiencing the risen Jesus personally which involves risk, trust, and commitment.

Jesus' own understanding at the beginning of his ministry is that his words and deeds would go together. He goes to his home synagogue and claims that the words of Isaiah are now fulfilled:

> *"The Spirit of the Lord is on me, because he has anointed me to proclaim good news to the poor. He has sent me to proclaim freedom for the prisoners and recovery of sight for the blind, to set the oppressed free, to proclaim the year of the Lord's favor."*
>
> Luke 4:18–19

These words set the scene for what is to happen in the rest of Luke's Gospel and indeed in what Luke records of the ministry of the followers of Jesus in Acts. The kingdom has arrived, characterized both by the preaching of good news to the needy and by the performance of mighty works. At the centre of the arrival of the kingdom is Jesus himself. Later in Luke's Gospel this is re-emphasized. In controversy with the Pharisees concerning the source of Jesus' power in casting out demons, Jesus replies that his casting out of demons is a sign of the presence of the kingdom (Luke 11:20).

Noticing that the miracles are not just an added extra but very much part of the story is very important for our understanding. C. S. Lewis wrote the following:

> *If you are writing a story, miracles or abnormal events may be bad art, or they may not. If, for example, you are writing an ordinary realistic novel and have got your characters into a hopeless muddle, it would be quite intolerable if you suddenly cut the knot and secured a happy ending by having the hero left a fortune from an unexpected quarter. On the other hand there is nothing against taking as your subject from the outset the adventures of a man who inherits an unexpected fortune... Some people probably think of the Resurrection as a desperate last moment expedient to save the Hero from a situation which had got out of the Author's control... [but] Death and Resurrection are what the story is about; and had we but eyes to see it, this has been hinted on every page, met us, in some disguise, at every turn, and even been muttered in conversations.*[35]

Such a view of the ministry of Jesus, and his continued encouragement to those who follow him, means that most Christians believe that God will be at work in them in a similar way to the ministry of Jesus. This gives a very strong mandate for Christians to pray for the miraculous.

---

35 Lewis, C. S. (1967). *Miracles: A Preliminary Study.* London: Fontana Books, p. 102.

As we noted earlier, there are some evangelical Christians who argue that miracles are not for today. They suggest that miracles were needed during the special time of Jesus and the apostles, to authenticate their message. Once the Bible was formed, there was no such need and therefore claims of modern miracles are either mistaken or frauds. Some support their case by referring to 1 Corinthians 13:8–10:

> But where there are prophecies, they will cease; where there are tongues they will be stilled; where there is knowledge, it will pass away. For we know in part and we prophesy in part, but when perfection comes, the imperfect disappears.

The argument is that now we have the Bible ("perfection") there is no need for signs such as tongues or prophecy. Now it is true that in the Bible miracles do seem to come in batches at particular points where they are needed, such as the deliverance from Egypt, the earthly life of Jesus, and the growth of the early church. However, that is not the whole story. There are "isolated miracles" throughout the Bible – for example the miracles of Elijah and Elisha (1 Kings 18; 2 Kings 5:1–15). In addition, what is surely referred to by "perfection" is that time when we see God "face to face" (1 Corinthians 13:12) – that is, the life to come. To write off the many miracles which have happened throughout the history of the church in many different cultures is a very dangerous, if not blasphemous, thing. Of course there will be occasions when the claims of miracles are mistaken. There will also be occasions of fraud. But we need to respect that God is sovereign in his will.

However, the eye-catching nature of the miraculous sometimes means that other biblical material is neglected.

The laws of nature in the Bible?

One of my favourite stories is of a young boy who was asked at his school to write an essay on birth. He went to his mother and asked how he was born, and she replied, "You came as a gift from God." He then asked his grandmother how his mother was born. She replied, "The stork brought her." He then asked his grandfather how his grandmother was born. He replied, "She was found under a gooseberry bush." When he handed in his essay it began with the words, "In my family, there has not been a natural birth for three generations!"

What is natural? What is a gift from God? And what do we really mean by "supernatural"? Basic to the biblical view is that all events are God's events. Creation is not seen as a mechanical model apart from God, which he makes and then waves goodbye. All events owe their existence to him. Therefore, for me as an astrophysicist, so-called "natural" events such as the sun shining (Matthew 5:45) are not only because of "the contraction of a ball of molecular hydrogen under gravity to a point where at the centre the temperature has risen so that nuclear fusion of the hydrogen into helium begins, thus halting the gravitational collapse while emitting photons of electromagnetic radiation which penetrate the atmosphere of the earth", but because of God's constant sustaining activity of the laws of gravity, quantum electrodynamics, and quantum chromodynamics which he initially provided. Whether it be grass growing (Psalm 104:14), rain falling (Matthew 5:45), mist rising (Jeremiah 10:13), or the path of the sun (Psalm 19:4–6), all are seen as part of God's sustaining activity. I do not find, therefore, the distinction between natural and supernatural helpful.

The laws of science are a description of God's regular activity in sustaining the universe. As I sit writing this paragraph on that wondrous thing called a laptop, the software gives to the screen and to the keys I press some regularity and order. The software enables me to see what I am writing and I know which parts of the screen to click on in order to change the font, the size, the background colour, and how to save all that I have been writing. For most of the time that I write, I do not think a lot about the software, but without it I would not be able to use this computer to write. If there was not a constancy to the software – that is, if it was changing all of the time – the task would be impossible. In fact, it is only when something unusual happens that I notice the software. If I press a key by accident which does something strange (like scrapping a whole day's work!), then I recognize the role of the software in maintaining the environment. I find this a helpful analogy in thinking about the laws of physics. Most of the time, I do not notice them or think about them, yet they structure my life within the universe.

God is the one who maintains the consistency of the laws of physics as they are a reflection of his upholding "the universe by the word of his power" (Hebrews 1:3). If God did not have a faithful relationship to the universe then there would be no patterns, no regularities, and no laws of physics. The universe would be a place of physical anarchy!

In the light of this, it is difficult to define miracles. The distinction between natural and supernatural seems to suggest some realms are where God works and some realms are not. For example, the atheist philosopher J. L. Mackie writes:

> *The laws of nature... describe the ways in which the world – including, of course, human beings – works when left to itself, when not interfered with. A miracle occurs when the world is not left to itself, when something distinct from the natural order as a whole intrudes into it.*[36]

Such a distinction is unknown to the biblical authors. However, on the basis of what we have seen from the Bible, we might broadly say that a miracle is something unusual which catches attention because of its nature or its timing and is intended by God to be a sign of his activity and power.

This is quite a contrast to what is the popular view – that a miracle is something scientifically impossible. In fact, the word "miracle" is not really a biblical word. It came out of the way that modern thinkers have tried to understand God's actions in relation to the regularity of the world disclosed by the Greek

36 Mackie, J. L. (1982). *The Miracle of Theism.* Oxford: Oxford University Press, pp.19–20.

philosophers, right through to the leaders of the scientific revolution. The term comes from the Latin word for wonder but increasingly became identified with an event which does not have a human or natural cause. Thus Thomas Aquinas (1225–74) defined a miracle as an event that exceeded the productive power of nature, but the philosopher David Hume (1711–76) defined it as a "violation" of the laws of nature.

Yet the three main biblical words used are "signs", "wonders", and "mighty works". Noting this, it frees us from seeing miracles as events of supernatural origins which break the scientific laws. The Bible encompasses a wider set of events. The order and vastness of the universe can be seen as signs of God's work which leads to wonder. The parting of the Red Sea, due to the wind, by the nature of its very special timing, is a mighty work which does not go against the laws of nature.

Miracles are those events that are intended by God to be special signs of the fact that he is present in the world and is in control of it. Scientists in astronomy are always dependent on others. Many observations are now done by satellites and the observations are "packaged" by a team of scientists often elsewhere in the world. That means that they send the observations and the computer software to display the data on the scientist's computer screen. Some years ago the data from one particular satellite had a little surprise to it. Occasionally and without warning, when one displayed the satellite's photograph of a particular part of the sky, a small silhouette of the Starship *Enterprise* appeared in the picture!

Assuming that this was not real (!), the team who had written the software had included in the program a routine which randomly displayed the *Enterprise*. It was certainly a reminder of who wrote the software!

In the light of this, we already begin to see that prayer that asks God to work in a special way within the universe has to take seriously his creation of and sustaining of the laws of physics which give the universe structure as well the diverse reasons for signs and wonders.

Miracles under attack!

For many people it is not enough to argue for the existence of miracles simply because the Bible says so. Strong arguments have been employed against miracles, many of which have been around for a long time. Some attempt to argue that miracles are in principle impossible, but there are also arguments which attempt to show that miracle claims could never be believable.[37] These arguments continue to be influential not only for belief in miracles but also for the question of how God answers when I pray.

First – and an argument that we have continually touched on – is that *God cannot work miracles in a scientific universe*. The scientific revolution disclosed a universe that was regular and predictable. Newton's law of gravitation, coupled with Kepler's elliptical orbits, was successful in explaining the movement of the planets around the sun. Although Newton himself did not

---

37 McGrew, T. (2013). "Miracles". *The Stanford Encyclopedia of Philosophy*. Zalta, E. N. (ed.): http://plato.stanford.edu/archives/spr2013/entries/miracles/

take this view, seeing the universe as a predictable clock is often called "the Newtonian worldview". The beauty, regularity, and simplicity of scientific laws were seen as reflections of the order and faithfulness of the creator God. But this in itself led to problems. If everything could be explained by scientific laws, was there space for God to do miracles? And if everything was perfect, having been created by God, why did God have to "correct the mechanism" of nature through miracles? Thus influential thinkers such as Voltaire, Spinoza, and Leibniz saw miracles as ugly cases where God would be acting against his own wisdom and violating the laws of nature. As Leibniz (1646–1716) wrote concerning nature, "I maintain it to be a watch, that goes without wanting to be mended by him."[38]

Second, *the evidence for miracles is never convincing.* One of the main critics of miracles was the Scottish philosopher David Hume.[39] He saw miracles as violations of the laws of nature. But the laws of nature are established by such a wealth of evidence and experience there simply will never be enough evidence to justify miracles. In a classic application of this, Hume writes of the resurrection:

> *When anyone tells me, that he saw a dead man restored to life, I immediately consider with myself, whether it be more probable, that this person should either deceive or be deceived, or that the fact, which he relates, should*

38 Alexander, H. G. (ed.) (1956). *The Leibniz-Clarke Correspondence.* Manchester: Manchester University Press, p.18.
39 Russell, P. (2013). "Hume on Religion". *The Stanford Encyclopedia of Philosophy.* Zalta, E. N. (ed.): http://plato.stanford.edu/archives/fall2013/entries/hume-religion/

> *really have happened. I weigh the one miracle against the*
> *other; and according to the superiority, which I discover,*
> *I pronounce my decision, and always reject the greater*
> *miracle. If the falsehood of his testimony would be more*
> *miraculous, than the event which he relates; then, and not*
> *till then, can he pretend to command my belief or opinion.*[40]

Philosophers continue to dispute the validity of such an argument, but the argument has filtered through into the popular consciousness coupled with a number of other Humean arguments. Hume suggests that miracles were not recorded by "men of good sense, education and learning" but by uncivilized people who knew no better and therefore could not be relied upon. In addition, he argues that people of religious commitment want to believe the evidence for miracles and indeed there is a general attraction in humans that we want to believe in events that produce feelings of surprise and wonder. Further, for Hume "a wise man proportions his belief to the evidence". As a miracle is rare compared with the evidence for the natural laws of science, then the miracle is not to be believed. Hume believes that in our knowledge of the world, our personal direct experience has priority and the testimony of others is only to be accepted if it fits with our experience. Therefore, as most of us have not had direct experience of a miracle, we cannot accept the testimony of others.

---

40 Hume, D. (1902). *An Enquiry Concerning Human Understanding*. Selby Bigge, L. A. (ed.). Oxford: Clarendon Press, p. 116.

It is a powerful critique of miracles. Yet we note at this stage it is completely dependent on the definition of a miracle as a violation of a law of nature. Further, the critique rests on the question of how evidence is used in proof and falsification. We should also observe that Hume uses such arguments primarily against those who would want to use miracles as a proof of the Christian message rather than ruling out the possibility of miracles.

Third, and perhaps most importantly, *it is a moral outrage that God only does some miracles and not others.* This is the theological question, "If God does work by miracle, then why does he not do it more often?" As we saw in Chapters 1 and 2 miracles are often claimed which at best seem trivial compared to the horrors of this world. James Keller in his book *Problems of Evil and the Power of God* sums up this moral argument: "It is unjust for God to perform miracles for some people and not for others, because in so doing God confers upon some people benefits that others with similar characteristics do not obtain."[41]

In fact it is this sort of question, the problem of evil, that has meant that a number of theologians have tried to suggest that God does not act at all in the world. By saying that God does no unusual or particular actions in the world, then God is "let off the hook" of why he did nothing in the particular case of, for example, the Holocaust.

---

41 Keller, J. (2007). *Problems of Evil and the Power of God.* London: Ashgate, p. 60.

The "de-miraclizing" of the New Testament

These three main problems lead to a questioning of the biblical stories. If science rules out the very possibility of miracles, then why are so many miracle stories reported in the Bible? Perhaps it is because the writers of the Bible were "uncivilized" people who wanted the story of Jesus to be true.

Two main options are given. The rationalists such as Heinrich Paulus (1761–1851) looked for natural explanations of what appeared to be miraculous. So the 5,000 were fed, not by a supernatural production of bread and fish, but by the crowd, motivated by the example of the small boy, getting out the bread and fish they had been saving for themselves. This approach has moved into much Christian preaching and teaching. In this way, Jesus the great teacher could be maintained and his '"miracles" were in affecting human beings' thoughts and actions. So the preacher could make the point of how we should all offer what we have in our bag for the benefit of Jesus and others! However, this kind of approach became extreme. Some have suggested that far from Jesus walking on the water he was in fact walking on a sandbank. It even suggests that the resurrection was in fact Jesus – who was not killed on the cross – being revived in the cool of the tomb.

I do not find this convincing in any way. It does not do justice to the accounts themselves or indeed the intelligence of the biblical witnesses. Would disciples who had fished on the Sea of Galilee for years mistake Jesus walking on a sandbank – or even worse, let the story of their mistake circulate around their friends and colleagues? Further, the feeding of the 5,000 is not presented in any of the Gospels as a parable to teach us to share our lunch with others. The focus of the story is the power of Jesus.

The other reinterpretation of the miracle stories was given by the German theologian David Friedrich Strauss in his influential *A New Life of Jesus*, published in 1879. This is to see the miracle stories as "myth" – that is, stories created from Old Testament patterns to convey a theological point about Jesus. Stories of Jesus doing miracles were created by the early church to express their beliefs about him. Thus, the resurrection did not actually happen; it is a story which tells us that what Jesus lived for will continue, a type of "Jesus' body lies a mouldering in his grave, but his truth goes marching on".

Strauss was followed by many in this programme of demythologizing the Bible. Ernst Troeltsch in 1898 introduced the principle of analogy, arguing that historical knowledge is only possible because all events are similar in principle. Therefore, we must assume that the laws of nature in biblical times were the same as now. This has been used by some biblical scholars to preclude any possibility of God doing anything special in the world. It has a touch of circularity of course. As science says that miracles cannot happen, then the evidence for miracles is unreliable and is dismissed. So a more modern scholar, Langdon Gilkey, writes:

> contemporary theology does not expect, nor does it speak
> of, wondrous divine events on the surface of natural and

historical life. The causal nexus in space and time which the
Enlightenment science and philosophy introduced into the
Western mind… is also assumed by modern theologians
and scholars; since they participate in the modern world
of science both intellectually and existentially, they can
scarcely do anything else. Now this assumption of a causal
order among phenomenal events, and therefore of the
authority of the scientific interpretation of observable
events, makes a great difference to the validity one assigns
to biblical narratives and so to the way one understands
their meaning. Suddenly a vast panoply of divine deeds
and events recorded in scripture are no longer regarded
as having actually happened… Whatever the Hebrews
believed, we believe that the biblical people lived in the
same causal continuum of space and time in which we live,
and so one in which no divine wonders transpired and no
divine voices were heard.[42]

This reading of the New Testament in particular continues
to be vastly influential today. It has also led to a number of
different models to try to understand how God works in the
world in the light of science and the problem of evil.

The "sit back and watch" God

One option is to simply accept the force of the problem of
evil and the mechanistic universe and to rule out completely
the ability of God to do anything in the world apart from his

---

42 Gilkey, L. (1983). "Cosmology, Ontology and the Travail of Biblical
Language". *God's Activity in the World: The Contemporary Problem.* Thomas, O.C.
(ed.). Chico, CA: Scholars Press, p. 31.

creating and sustaining of the physical laws. In this way God does not do anything when I pray.

Such an approach was taken by the Oxford theologian Maurice Wiles. His book *God's Action in the World* was rather cruelly nicknamed in my student days as *God's Inaction in the World*. Wiles argues that God's action is limited to that one great single act which caused and keeps the universe in being. It is an act that allows radical freedom to human creatures and indeed radical self-limitation on God's part.[43]

His analogy is that of an improvised drama. The author gives basic characters and the setting. The resulting drama may follow the intention of the author, but the actors have freedom to determine their own outcome. The actors may request help from the author, but in order to give them their own complete freedom the author does not get involved. Evil becomes the risk taken by God in allowing freedom to life within a physical lawful environment. Prayer is thus simply a way of recognizing and giving thanks to God for the gift of creation.

Now, it is reasonable that if God is at work in the world then part of its expression will certainly be found in the reliability and beauty of the laws of nature. Indeed, as we have seen, this is part of the biblical view. In our desperation of asking for things we sometimes forget the importance and joy of thanking God for the structure of the world. This has often been focused in Christian liturgy in thankfulness for the seasons and in particular the festival of harvest. There is something about recognizing in this the faithfulness of God

---

43 Wiles, M. (1986). *God's Action in the World*. London: SCM Press.

which has also become a source of confidence for the future. Thus the hymn "Great is thy faithfulness" celebrates:

> *Summer and winter, and springtime and harvest,*
> *Sun, moon and stars in their courses above,*
> *Join with all nature in manifold witness*
> *To Thy great faithfulness, mercy and love*[44]

As a scientist, I do wonder that if in our prayer we so rush towards the miraculous that we do not give enough attention to thankfulness for creation. It is rare when I find myself in church being led to thank God for the gift of genetics. As well as the natural seasons I would like to see more churches thank God for the gift of science, with the associated joy of exploring and shaping the world.

I have encountered many scientists within Christian churches who sense that their work is a calling from God, but do not feel that the church recognizes or values this calling. This needs church leaders who are wise to see that God calls not only missionaries but also mechanical engineers. But I also feel it is a reminder of the importance of keeping thanksgiving and petition in a good balance in personal and public prayer. In thanksgiving and praise we can highlight God's faithfulness and the beauty of the world, and this gives an important context for asking God then to act in special ways in the world.

---

44 Taken from "Great Is Thy Faithfulness" by Thomas O. Chisholm © 1923. Ren. 1951 Hope Publishing Company, Carol Stream, IL 60188, www.hopepublishing. com All rights reserved. Used by permission.

For John Wesley this was at the heart of prayer:

> *Thanksgiving is inseparable from true prayer; it is almost*
> *essentially connected with it. One who always prays is ever*
> *giving praise, whether in ease or pain, both for prosperity*
> *and for the greatest adversity. He blesses God for all things,*
> *looks on them as coming from Him, and receives them for*
> *His sake – not choosing nor refusing, liking or disliking*
> *anything, but only as it is agreeable or disagreeable to His*
> *perfect will.*[45]

In addition, we have to agree that God must have a consistent rather than fitful relationship with creation. Wiles stresses the way God sustains the world and this is helpful. We can also sympathize with Wiles' motive to take seriously the problem of evil. His solution – that God simply cannot do anything about it – is not new and remains an option which needs to be examined.

However, the model has some major weaknesses. First, a God who does nothing particular in the universe makes it difficult to see how God can be spoken of in terms of personal relationships. What is the difference to the actors between a playwright who never responds and one who is dead? A God who does nothing in particular in the universe might as well be an impersonal mathematical equation.

Second, Wiles' treatment of the biblical material follows the Strauss line and thus he is at pains to interpret both the

---

45 John Wesley's Bible Commentary Notes, http://wesley.nnu.edu/john-wesley/john-wesleys-notes-on-the-bible/notes-on-st-pauls-first-epistle-to-the-thessalonians/.

incarnation and resurrection as non-miraculous events. A God who does nothing particular cannot become flesh and cannot raise someone from the dead. Thus Wiles takes the view that these stories are created to express theological truth, although it is difficult to know on this picture why this is needed.

Third, Wiles' whole view of science is based on the Newtonian mechanistic universe. The next chapter will show that this is out of date. If this is the case, then a "sit back and watch" God becomes much less appealing.

For these reasons I have not found this model convincing.

The "working in the mind" God

One of the foremost New Testament scholars who followed on from Strauss was Rudolf Bultmann (1884–1976). Bultmann, like Wiles, saw science describing the universe in completely Newtonian mechanistic terms. On this basis he was concerned for theological integrity both within the Christian faith and in how that faith was communicated to others:

> We cannot use electric lights and radios and in the event of illness avail ourselves of modern medical and clinical means and at the same time believe in the spirit and wonder world of the New Testament. And if we suppose that we can do so ourselves, we must be clear that we can represent this as the attitude of Christian faith only by making the Christian proclamation unintelligible and impossible for our contemporaries.[46]

46 Bultmann, R. (1984). *New Testament & Mythology*. Minneapolis, MN: Augsburg Fortress, pp. 4–5.

He developed an existentialist approach in which he therefore drew a distinction between the "exterior" world of science and the "interior" world of religion, in that there is a fundamental difference in our knowledge of physical events compared to the God who is known in experience. God does not act in the physical world in any particular physical way, but achieves his purposes by "acting" in the person of faith as he or she encounters God's Word.[47] This means that as one encounters the living God – for example in the pages of the Bible – God can act in that person. Prayer for the end of a drought will not lead to God making it rain, but to the praying person being moved to help. Søren Kierkegaard (1813–55) expressed this view in his famous quotation, "The function of prayer is not to influence God, but rather to change the nature of the one who prays."

The merit of this kind of view is clear. It respects the scientific laws and puts the moral responsibility for doing something about the problem of evil onto the human agent rather than upon God. The fact that the human agent is not totally good means that evil is left unopposed and indeed is caused by the human agent. A sense of a loving and living God is maintained.

However, can such a fundamental distinction between exterior and interior worlds be made? Such a view seems to reflect Greek dualism, which distinguishes between the

---

47   Bultmann, R. (1983). "The Meaning of God as Acting". *God's Activity in the World: The Contemporary Problem*. Thomas, O. C. (ed.). Chico, CA: Scholars Press.

physical and the spiritual, which is far from the way the Hebrew context of the Bible sees the psychosomatic of the human person. Some critics have suggested that even a model of God changing a person's mind implies some particular interaction of God with the physical world. After all, would God not have to actually change the electrical currents in the neurones of my brain in order for me to give money to a charity to alleviate hunger and poverty?

Due to developments in cognitive neuroscience in the last twenty years, which has brought together experimental psychology, comparative neuropsychology, and brain imaging techniques, this may be less of a problem than was originally thought. The relationship between mind and brain is at the centre of this area of science. Its relevance reaches not only to medical and psychological treatment but also to questions such as what makes human beings different from animals and the emerging intellectual processing power of artificial intelligence. It is leading, in the words of Professor of Psychology Malcolm Jeeves, to an increasing appreciation of the "irreducible interdependence of mind and brain".[48] That is, the mind and the brain are inextricably linked. This can be shown in two complementary ways.

The first is what is called "bottom up evidence", which shows that changes in the brain affect the mind. This was initially realized due to injuries to the brain either in warfare

---

48 Jeeves, M. (2004). "Mind Reading and Soul Searching in the Twenty-First Century: The Scientific Evidence". *What About the Soul? Neuroscience and Christian Anthropology*. Green, J. B. (ed.). Nashville: Abingdon, pp.13–30.

or accidents. The classic example is that of Phineas Gage, a supervisor on a railway construction team in 1848. Due to an accidental explosion a metal bar was propelled and lodged in the frontal part of Gage's brain, destroying much of his left frontal lobe. Surprisingly, he survived and indeed remained conscious. However, more significantly, when the bar had been removed and Gage had physically recovered, his personality had changed dramatically. Previously he had been conscientious, reliable, a hard-working pillar of society, and committed to his family. After the accident he became an unreliable, boastful gambler unable to concentrate or hold down a job. No doubt part of this can be put down to the trauma of the accident, but those who studied his case saw that the damage to his brain had literally changed his mind.

Yet alongside this, there is also "top down" evidence of the relationship between mind and brain. For example, the training of the mind can lead to physical changes in the brain. MRI scans show that taxi drivers, who have to learn the "All-London Knowledge" of streets and landmarks, increase the size of their posterior hippocampus at the base of the brain. Their brain structure is modified by their mental processes.

Now, as philosopher and theologian Nancey Murphy rightly points out, this tightening of the mind/brain link in neurobiology makes it more improbable for such an ontologically separate entity as the soul to exist.[49] It is important to be clear about what is meant when Christians

---

49 Murphy, N. (2000). "Science and Society". *Systematic Theology*, Vol 3: Witness. McClendon, J. W and Murphy, N. (eds). Nashville: Abingdon, pp. 99–131.

claim such things. For many people within Christianity the language of soul is often shorthand to express our spiritual capacity of relating to God. I agree with Murphy and others that modern science does not give room for a distinct entity called the soul; however, this does not mean that I deny the spiritual capacity of relating to God. I believe that God relates to the whole of the human person rather than just a "god-receiver" which mysteriously resides somewhere within us.

This understanding of the tightening mind/brain link does open the door a little wider for how God might change the human person in the prayer encounter. The God who speaks through spiritual disciplines of meditation, fasting, praise, Bible reading, and confession, which renew the mind, can therefore change the structure of the brain. This could give a coherent understanding of how God responds in prayer by changing the one who prays. Indeed, the regular rhythms of such spiritual disciplines can shape both psychological and physical structures within the brain.

However, does such a view really make sense of the richness of the biblical story? It is dependent on a view that rules out God interacting directly with the physical world and the demythologization of the Bible by Strauss and others. If the accounts of the Bible are taken at face value, they do speak of incidents where the person who prays is led to do something that changes the course of history. The book of Acts is full of such instances of dreams and visions in prayer leading to particular actions. Ananias is sent to the young convert Saul who would become Paul (Acts 9:10–17), and Peter is changed in his attitude to Gentiles (Acts 10). Yet these incidents are interwoven with physical healings (Acts 9:18; 14:8–10) and miraculous escapes from prisons (Acts 11; 16:25–40). Luke records all of these incidents without distinction in style or genre.

Prayer certainly is about a fundamental encounter with God which changes a human person. And it is certainly one way that God responds to prayer by using changed human beings to be partners in building the kingdom. But there is more to it than just this.

For this reason I am again unconvinced by this model. I do think it is valuable in understanding that part of prayer is the transformation in a fundamental way of the person who prays. But it limits God's freedom and power too much.

A "persuasive" God

The strict adherence to a Newtonian worldview and its ruling out of any significant interaction between God and the natural world, although dominant in many intellectual circles, was not universal. A purely mechanistic universe not only rules out God's freedom to do anything, it also rules out the reality of human free will. In his Gifford Lectures of 1927, *Process and Reality,* Alfred North Whitehead opened up a new model for thinking about God's relationship with the world by introducing a new metaphysics. (This is a philosophical understanding of the world which is not testable by science.) Reality is seen as a process, in dynamic rather than static terms, with the central metaphor being that of biological organism rather than machine.

It attempts to proceed by assimilating the nature of the universe to our nature. Our nature could be understood as a combination of the material and the mental, with each giving both opportunity and constraint. For example, in my mind I would love to play football like Lionel Messi, but as a right-footed, overweight 51-year-old I am somewhat constrained!

Process thinkers thus suggest each event in the universe has a material pole and a psychic or subjective pole. As this is extended to theology, so process theologians use an analogy between God's action and our experience as agents. Thus it was suggested God is dipolar, consisting of a consequent or responsive nature – affected by experience of all other entities – and a primordial constant nature. God works as an agent at the subjective level, exercising power by persuasion or lure rather than coercion. Further, just as we exist, influencing and being influenced by others, so God has a genuine relationship with creation where he also is influenced.

The attraction of this is that God is able to lure the physical while interacting with the "spiritual". This helps lessen the problem of evil, in that it creates a "free process" defence. The free will defence of the problem of evil is well known: God is not responsible for evil which comes as a result of the choices of human free will. But process theology says that all events in the universe (whether involving human beings or not) have some capacity for free choice. Thus the very physical processes are not bound to respond to God – they can decide to go their own way. God is thus absolved of the blame for both natural and moral evil, and indeed becomes a fellow sufferer who understands our pain.

Popular in the 1960s and 1970s, process theology seems strange to many contemporary people. Its metaphysics is very different to our usual way of viewing the world. It presents God rather like a teacher or parent – not completely outside the universe, intimately related to the universe, but only able to influence through persuasion. Thus, God's ability to respond to prayer which asks for something to be changed in the world is rather like me asking my teenage daughter to tidy up her bedroom. I cannot force her to do it; I can only persuade and occasionally bribe!

However, a number of problems have been raised. First, there is no evidence that the physical world has such a nature, and it is unclear how the psychic and material poles are connected. Second, it is difficult to make sense of the implication that even primitive objects such as quarks have an ability to "select" outcomes. Third, it is difficult to see how God can do anything of importance at such a level. Is God reduced to as passive a deity as Wiles' creator? As the theologian E. L. Mascall once commented, process theology can mean our "final attitude to God is not one of adoration so much as sympathy".[50]

Yet, some of the insights of process theology are helpful.

---

50 Mascall, E. L. (1966). *He who is*. London: DLT, p. 157.

In any sense of how God answers prayer the "responsiveness and resistance" of creation to the Spirit of God need to be taken into account.[51] Perhaps God decides to limit the exercise of his own power in order to give a degree of genuine freedom. We will return to this insight in the next chapter.

A "bodily" God

There is one more model, which has achieved some supporters, that we need to explore before we leave this chapter. "Panentheism" uses an analogy between God's action and our action but attempts to assimilate God's action in the world to our action in our bodies. Grace Jantzen sees the world as God's body, God working in it just as the soul works within the body.[52] In a similar way Arthur Peacocke views the universe as a foetus in the "womb" of God.[53] Thus God can act on any part of the world in a way similar to our action on our bodies, but God also is greater than the world.

Such an approach has attraction, not least in holding together both the immanence of God and the transcendence of God. God is greater than the universe but is intimately involved in it. However, I do not find this a very helpful model for understanding prayer or how God actually works in the world. First, we do not understand enough about embodiment in order to use such an analogy. Even if we believe in a separate

---

51 Fiddes, P. (1993). "Process Theology". *The Blackwell Encyclopaedia of Modern Christian Thought*. McGrath, A. (ed.). Oxford: Blackwell, pp. 472–476.
52 Jantzen, G. (1984). *God's World, God's Body*. London: DLT.
53 Peacocke, A. (2001). *Paths from Science Towards God: The End of All Our Exploring*. Oxford: Oneworld.

soul, how does "the soul work in the body"? Mothers sustain the baby in their womb but do not act on it in particular ways. It is difficult to see whether this is any different from a "sit back and watch" God with more attention paid to the commitment God gives in sustaining the universe. Second, if the universe is in some way God's body, then does God become vulnerable as the universe changes with time? The analogy is very good at 13.8 billion years when the universe has order and discernible structure, but is totally inappropriate when the universe is a quark soup. And what was God like before the Big Bang? Third, such an analogy sees the nature of the physical world as an organism having unity to its overall structure. But the universe is just too subtle to fit the picture. In some senses it shows "organism" qualities, in other senses "mechanistic" qualities, and in other senses "chaotic" qualities, of which we will say more in a moment. It is a subtle admixture of many things. Fourth, it can be argued that panentheism threatens God's otherness and freedom, but also compromises the world's freedom to be itself.

Moving on into at least the twentieth century

The models of this chapter are rooted in the scientific worldview of Newton which has shaped theology and indeed objections to God's responding to prayer in specific physical ways in the world. They have heavily influenced biblical interpretation and sent theologians looking for models which are consistent with such a view.

But there is a fundamental problem with all of this. Science is no longer stuck in the pre-twentieth-century world of Newton. Indeed, in 1986, 300 years after *Principia Mathematica* was presented to the Royal Society, the International Union of Theoretical and Applied Mechanics made a public apology:

> *We collectively wish to apologize for having misled the general educated public by spreading ideas about the determinism of systems satisfying Newton's laws of motion that, after 1960, were proved to be incorrect... Modern theories of dynamical systems have clearly demonstrated the unexpected fact that systems governed by the equations of Newtonian dynamics do not necessarily exhibit the "predictability" property.*[54]

This is an extraordinary statement and it would be helpful that here in the twenty-first century theologians at least caught up with the science of the last century! We will attempt to do this in the next chapter and discover that the world of contemporary science opens up new possibilities. That is not to say that we will find easy solutions, but we will discover an arena of theological thinking with fewer constraints.

---

54 Lighthill, J. (1986). "The Recently Recognized Failure of Predictability in Newtonian Dynamics". *Proceedings of the Royal Society of London*, A407, 38, 35.

CHAPTER 5

New Science and New Possibilities

Science searches for patterns in the world. We call those patterns the laws of nature. They describe to us what normally does happen. The writer on science and faith Michael Poole helpfully likens scientific laws to a map of how the land lies. As the lie of the land determines the shape of the map, so our observations of the universe determine the form of the laws. He goes on to contrast this with an architect's plans. These plans are not descriptive but prescriptive in that they show what ought to take place. Many people make the mistake of seeing scientific laws as an architect's plans, telling us what should or should not happen. Of course they do have the ability on the basis of what happened before to lead us to expect certain things, but they do not make these things happen. The map has to be changed by what is really there.

The Babylonians were probably the first to attempt to map the world in the ninth century BC. Then, during the Age of Exploration from the fifteenth to the seventeenth centuries, map making went forward at a renewed pace due to observation and inventions such as the magnetic compass and the sextant. However, it was the advent of aerial and satellite imagery that allowed precise methods to be used for everything from coastlines to buildings, and a new accuracy in description. While contemporary maps do not change substantially, they still have to be constantly updated as features change.

Nevertheless, the maps of today are very different to the Babylonian maps or even more recent maps. Until the time of the great exploration of the interior of Africa, the continent was mapped around its edges, but the vast majority of the continent remained a mystery to maps of the time. The mistake of many is to think that Newton gave us a pretty near perfect picture of how the world is – an unchanging, accurate, and exhaustive map. In fact, even with the considerable scientific advances up to the end of the nineteenth century there were large parts that were waiting to be discovered. The implications of this are both puzzling and profound.

From clocks to clouds

Quantum theory was developed in the early part of the twentieth century and deals with the world at the level of atoms and the particles such as protons, neutrons, and electrons which form them. It is one of the most powerful theories of modern physics, giving the world lasers, nuclear power, the transistor, and the electron microscope. It has also helped us to understand the conduction of electricity, the structure of the atom, and perhaps, in the future, the very beginning of the universe.

Newton's world was the universe as a predictable clock or machine with laws which describe well such systems as the orbits of the planets. By knowing the present position of an object and its movement we can predict where it will be in the future. The world is picturable, reliable, and determined.

However, in the small-scale structure of the world described by quantum theory, that is far from the truth. The world is not picturable or determined. For example, I can catch a cricket ball because I can see its position and its velocity as it moves towards me. But for the fundamental particles which make up all of matter this is not the case. For example, we can know either the position of an electron or its movement, but we cannot have both. This is expressed in the Heisenberg Uncertainty Principle and can be thought about in terms of the electron having a probability of being in a range of locations. In the words of particle physicist and Anglican priest John Polkinghorne, this means that the quantum world is "radically random". By that he means it is unpredictable and nothing like a mechanical clock. It is a world that is unpicturable, uncertain, and in which the cause of events cannot be fully specified.

This is a world that is completely counterintuitive but one that is experimentally verified. Quantum theory works. Yet there remain, even after a century of work on quantum theory, two unanswered questions. The first is the measurement problem: how is it that the uncertain quantum world gives predictable, measurable answers when interrogated by our macro world? After all, the cricket ball is made up of atoms made up of electrons, protons, and neutrons. To use the uncertainty of electrons as an excuse for a dropped catch is not convincing! How does the world of probabilities connect with the everyday world of certainty? There are a number of options. One is that the intervention of macro-world measuring instruments "collapses" the probability in one definite measurement. The vast majority of quantum physicists, including one of its founders, Niels Bohr, take this option, named the Copenhagen interpretation. However, such an interpretation poses the puzzle of how this happens, as the very measuring instruments are themselves composed of atoms which have quantum behaviour. A second option attempts to get around this problem by saying that it is the intervention of a conscious observer that leads to a measurement. It is not until the mind becomes involved that an answer becomes definite. Yet the same problem arises, as the brain itself is composed of atoms. A third interpretation is somewhat bizarre but is preferred by some cosmologists attempting to apply quantum theory to the universe as a whole where there are no measuring instruments or conscious observers. This is Hugh Everett III's Many Worlds interpretation. In every act of measurement, each possibility available is realized and at that point the universe splits into separate universes corresponding to the realized possibilities.

This leads to an unimaginable number of universes. Other options exist and there remains no consensus on the best interpretation.

The second unanswered question is, what does quantum theory actually tell us about the nature of reality? A minority led by David Bohm see the theory as simply a calculational procedure telling us nothing of the actual nature of atoms. One day we will discover deeper theory, so called "hidden variables". Einstein tended to think in this way, disliking the random nature of quantum theory with his famous dictum, "God does not play dice with the universe." However, the vast majority of physicists see the uncertainty not as ignorance on our part, but written into the fundamental nature of reality. This latter position is the one that I find most convincing.

Now what might this say to our question of when I pray, how does God answer? The first and most important consequence of quantum theory is simply that the Newtonian picture of the world is far from being a good picture of the world. Unless one takes the minority Bohm interpretation of quantum theory, this theory is telling us that a world modelled on a clock is far, far from the truth. The implications of this are profound. Remember we saw that the opposition to miracles and the subsequent demythologizing of the New Testament was predicated on this Newtonian worldview. It is just a pity that theologians did not pick this up when quantum theory appeared in the 1920s! At the very least quantum theory makes us extremely sceptical of the whole edifice of theological scholarship built on what now appears to be a very limited and small description of the world.

I have often wondered why so many of my fellow theologians seem stuck in Newtonian physics. It is true that quantum physics is difficult to fully get to grips with if you do not understand the language of mathematics which underlies its formulation. Theologians cannot be experts in everything. But there is perhaps a deeper reason. Some decades ago chemist and commentator C. P. Snow spoke about the "two cultures" of Western education and thinking. He pointed out the cultural separation of science and humanities and, in his view, the dominance in general culture of arts and humanities rather than science. In a classic quote he expressed his frustration at this:

> A good many times I have been present at gatherings of people who, by the standards of the traditional culture, are thought highly educated and who have with considerable gusto been expressing their incredulity at the illiteracy of scientists. Once or twice I have been provoked and have asked the company how many of them could describe the Second Law of Thermodynamics. The response was cold: it was also negative. Yet I was asking something which is the scientific equivalent of: Have you read a work of Shakespeare's? I now believe that if I had asked an even simpler question – such as, What do you mean by mass, or acceleration, which is the scientific equivalent of saying, Can you read? – not more than one in ten of the highly educated would have felt that I was speaking the same

language. So the great edifice of modern physics goes up,
and the majority of the cleverest people in the western
world have about as much insight into it as their neolithic
ancestors would have had.[55]

Snow may be overly harsh, but I am challenged by the importance of bringing scientists and theologians into genuine discussion and mutual learning. It seems to me that part of our limitations in thinking about prayer is that we have not done enough of this.

The second consequence of quantum theory is whether the unpredictability of the quantum world gives freedom to God to work within the scientific laws of the universe in unusual ways. Sir John Eccles was one of the first to pick up on this possibility, arguing that the uncertainty of the quantum world gave the space for human free will. Then, in the 1950s, William Pollard argued that this uncertainty may be the locus of God's free and "cloaked" action in the world.[56] God has the freedom to "push" an electron here or there and alter the course of events in the world, without breaking any of the laws of nature.

Unfortunately, the problem of this suggestion is that it involves one of the big unanswered questions of quantum theory which we noted earlier. How does the quantum world

55 Snow, C. P. (1969). *The Two Cultures and a Second Look: An Expanded Version of the Two Cultures and the Scientific Revolution.* Cambridge: Cambridge University Press., p.14–15.
56 Pollard, W. G. (1958). *Chance and Providence: God's Action in a World Governed by Scientific Law.* New York: Charles Scribner's Sons.

relate to the everyday world? It is difficult to see how God working at the uncertainty of the quantum level would affect the everyday level. To continue the sporting illustrations, a golf ball is made of atoms, but the laws that determine its flight are not the uncertainty of quantum theory but the certainty of Newton. It does have a very small probability of spontaneously disappearing in mid-flight, but that is never observed (contrary to the claims of some golfers who should be looking more intently in the rough!).

Nevertheless, it remains a possibility for a type of divine action which can respond to prayer while remaining consistent with the laws of physics. Some have tried to use quantum theory as giving a mechanism by which God performs miracles. But the whole point about miracles in the Bible is that they are not about God's hidden action. They are in fact quite the opposite, drawing attention directly to God's special actions in the world for specific purposes.

There is a third consequence of quantum theory which may seem trivial but is worth noting. It breaks what John Polkinghorne calls the "tyranny of common sense". So many theological models of how God acts fall under this tyranny. Now this is not to say that anything goes or that we hide behind "it's all mysterious", but it does mean that we should be careful in imposing our expectations or experiences on to how God acts in the universe. In fact, an example of this in quantum theory also demonstrates yet more relationality at the heart of the physical world. In 1935, Einstein, with his collaborators

Podolsky and Rosen, highlighted what they believed was an unacceptable consequence of quantum theory. In this EPR paradox, they pointed out that two quantum particles such as electrons, once they have interacted with each other, retain the ability to influence each other even though extremely large distances separate them. Einstein felt this showed that quantum theory was incomplete. Yet observations have confirmed that this really happens. What the experiment demonstrates is that at the quantum level, there is, in Polkinghorne's phrase, "togetherness in separation". This is unexpected and unexplained and yet is part of the way the world is. It may indicate that relationality is a fruitful way of thinking more about God's interaction with the universe. Now this example does not necessarily provide a mechanism for how God influences electrons; it simply says that the old mechanistic universe does not represent the world as it really is. Further, it gives a glimpse that the processes of physics need to be understood not in isolation but within a much bigger context.

I am not convinced that quantum theory gives an exhaustive and fully convincing way to reconcile God's answering of prayer with a scientific worldview. However, it may be one dimension of how God works in the world. It offers a tantalizing pointer that relationality is part of the physicality of the world, something that is at the heart of prayer.

The chaos of clouds

Chaos is one of the other great insights of twentieth-century physics. Unlike quantum theory, this theory deals not with matter at the atomic level but with things at an everyday level similar to Newton's theories. What it has helped us to see is that, even excluding quantum theory, Newton's laws themselves are not able to predict the future in the way we thought. The full implications of chaos theory have only been brought out in the latter part of the century, mainly due to the advent of computers able to do high-speed calculations.

When we look at problems to solve we begin with the easy ones and work up towards the difficult ones. When Newton published his monumental work *Principia* in 1686, he applied his new theory of gravitation to a reasonably simple system, which is two bodies such as the earth's motion around the sun. It is simple because we can get an exact answer.

Unfortunately, most of the rest of the world is not that simple. Most systems in the world are extremely sensitive to the circumstances around them, so much so that the slightest disturbance will make them act in a radically different way. This means that after a short time a system becomes essentially unpredictable.

A classic example of this occurred as early as 1961 in the work of Edward Lorenz, a meteorology professor at MIT.[57] Lorenz was interested in air movements in the atmosphere and was trying to model them through mathematical equations

57 Lorenz, E. N. (1963). "Deterministic Nonperiodic Flow". *Journal of the Atmospheric Sciences*, 20, pp. 130–141.

and a computer. He would type in the starting conditions; the computer would solve the equations and give a prediction. In one of these computer runs he typed in a number that was just slightly wrong by only one part in a thousand. His common sense told him that this small error would cause only a very small difference in the final prediction but, much to his surprise, he found that this small error in the starting conditions changed the prediction enormously. What he had come across was a chaotic system. Chaotic systems exhibit a great sensitivity to initial conditions, with very different outcomes arising from infinitesimally different starting points. The phenomenon became known as "the butterfly effect" after Lorenz gave a lecture in 1979 entitled, "Predictability; does the flap of a butterfly's wings in Brazil set off a tornado in Texas?".

The weather is a chaotic system. The physical laws that determine the weather are well known, and forecasters use these to make weather predictions. Why, then, do they get things wrong, and why do forecasts get more inaccurate the further ahead they predict? Chaos explains this by saying that even if the laws are known, accurate predictions are extremely sensitive to the initial conditions. Even if scientists collect excellent data on pressure and temperature to start off their predictions, there will always be a degree of uncertainty. This uncertainty is amplified in a chaotic system.

Now we need to note an important feature. While detailed predictions of whether it will rain on a particular day in a particular place in three weeks' time become impossible, chaotic systems do have the property that certain gross features such as global warming can be predicted. Sir John Houghton, former Chief Executive of the Meteorological Office and co-chairman of the scientific group of the Intergovernmental Panel on Climate Change, writes the following:

> *Even if we could observe the state of the atmosphere all over the globe much more accurately than present… forecasts of detailed weather conditions would be possible at most some two or three weeks into the future. But forecasts of the average weather or climate, at least in some parts of the world, may be possible much further ahead. And despite the frightening complexity of the whole system, we also have good reason to expect that useful predictions can be made of the likely climatic change due to human activities.*[58]

These words are important to bear in mind. While acknowledging that detailed predictions are out, Houghton is saying that does not mean you can say nothing about the future. Some recent philosophers and theologians have made the mistake of saying that chaos means the future is fully "open" – that is, we can know nothing about it. That is not correct. We can predict certain things about the future, whether it be chaotic systems or simple systems, but chaos reminds us of the severe limitations of those predictions.

Yet there is a sneaking suspicion in some of us that if only we had a big enough computer then we would be able

---

58 Houghton, J. T. (1995). *The Search for God: Can Science Help?* Oxford: Lion, p. 81.

to predict a system fully. It is worth pressing this question. We can illustrate this by balls moving on a snooker table. Great snooker players win their matches on the basis of Newton's view of the world. After having hit the cue ball, the balls eventually come to rest because of the friction of the table, the cushions, and the balls themselves. But imagine if there was no friction, and after the player made his break at the beginning of a frame we simply let the balls continue to collide into each other and the cushions. Our task would be to calculate, using the vast computer that we have brought along with us to the snooker hall, where all the balls would be after just one minute. If you know a little bit about mathematics you might think this is fairly easy. Once you knew the force with which the cue ball was hit, in the case of no friction, you would assume it would be an easy task, more suited to your home personal computer.

You would be wrong. This system – that is, the balls moving on a table – is a chaotic system. The staggering answer is that to accurately predict the position of the balls after only one minute, you need to take into account effects as small as the gravitational attraction (the weakest force) of an electron (the smallest particle) on the edge of the galaxy which is some 1,000,000,000,000,000 kilometres away![59] This illustrates very easily that you come up against two constraints in being able to predict a system. The first is that you would need to build a computer bigger than the universe itself to take into account all of these effects. The second is that there is of course a natural

---

59 Crutchfield, J.P. et al. (1986). "Chaos". *Scientific American* 255, p. 38.

limit on specifying the initial conditions and that is, as we saw in the previous section, the uncertainty of quantum theory.

Now, what are the consequences of chaos for our theological thinking? First, and most importantly, just like quantum theory it completely undermines the Newtonian paradigm of the predictable clock-like world and all of the theological systems built upon it. While we might not get an easy answer to how God answers prayer, at least we know that many of the arguments of the past and indeed present opposing God working in the world are simply wrong. Chaos perhaps is even more significant than quantum theory because it is about systems not at the microscopic scale but at the macro scale.

Second, such systems are never truly isolated. This is important in opposing a view called reductionism – the view that if you can understand the components of a system you can then understand the behaviour of the system as a whole. Reductionism underlies thinkers such as Dawkins, who claim that once the science of the universe is understood that is all you need. In fact, complex systems such as chaotic systems are a reminder that when components get together in relationship new phenomena emerge which cannot be reduced to the components themselves.

Third, we need to take care and acknowledge that not all systems are chaotic and some simple systems remain, such as the motion of the earth around the sun, where the Newtonian picture is still valid. In the words of philosopher Karl Popper, the world contains both clocks and clouds. In thinking about how God works in the world, we need to take seriously this diverse world. Maybe God's way of interacting with the world in answer to prayer is also diverse?

Fourth, just as we asked in regard to quantum theory, does chaos give space for God to work in unusual and specific ways within the scientific description of the world? Chaotic systems have a great advantage over quantum systems in that their effects are felt at the everyday level. Once again, it does depend on the crucial question of whether chaos is indicating that there is a fundamental openness to the world, or whether the world is determined but we just cannot see it. Polkinghorne has argued strongly that it is the former and chaos indicates that there is an openness in the world – the future is not totally determined.[60] That is, the universe is inherently open to the future, unpredictable and undetermined. This then gives "space" for human freedom. The reality of human freedom is thus maintained in a world described by science and further can be used to explain the source of some evil in the world. This free will defence suggests that some evil is caused by the bad choices of human beings and is a consequence of the possibility of free will. In a similar way, the openness to the future of chaos also gives space for a "free process defence" for natural evil. That is, in systems where human beings' free choices cannot be the cause of evil, it may be that the openness that the universe has in exploring its potential can sometimes be for good and sometimes for evil. Further, Polkinghorne

---

60 Polkinghorne, J. C. (1989). *Science and Providence*. London: SPCK.

suggests that God is at work in the flexibility of these open systems as well as being the ground of law. God's particular activity is real, but it is hidden.

This means that we can pray and God responds by working in the openness of a chaotic system. So Polkinghorne suggests that we can pray for rain, as the weather is a chaotic system, but it would be wrong to pray for spring to follow summer, as the seasons are determined by the simple system of the earth's orbit around the sun. In this way, God does not have problems with "breaking his own laws". Because these systems are unpredictable God could work while being undetectable. He could provide an unexpected lightning flash on York Minster while not compromising the physics of weather forecasting.

I find again great value in some of these insights. They present a world of subtlety, relationality, and a future that is not determined. In response to Einstein's "God does not play dice", Stephen Hawking, in a different context, commented, "God does play dice, and sometimes he throws them where we can't see." It does give God a possible avenue for interacting with the physical world independent from his interaction with human beings without being detected. The mathematician Ian Stewart commented, "If God played dice he would win"![61]

Yet, the weakness of such a position is saying that God can work only in chaotic systems and not in other ways. I worry that this limits the sovereignty of God. Is this a limit to God's omnipotence which actually undermines traditional

---

61 Stewart, I. (1989). *Does God Play Dice?* Oxford: Blackwell.

Christian theism, or, as we will return to later, does God *self-limit* the acts that he performs in the universe? Might he choose to exercise his freedom to act only in the uncertainty of chaotic systems? There are some biblical pointers that God does limit the freedom that he has. For example, following the flood at the time of Noah, God promises "Never again will all life be destroyed by the waters of a flood" (Genesis 9:11). Omnipotence is maintained if God is the one who self-limits his actions, rather than being constrained by a greater power or unable to do something because he is not powerful enough. I think this is a way of thinking about God's activity which is consistent with science and gives some way forward to responding to the problem of evil. God can work in particular ways in some systems in the world but may choose not to work in others.

However, it does seem a little arbitrary in drawing a line of what God can do and what he cannot do on the basis of a certain current scientific understanding of the world. This is exactly what was done on the basis of Newton's understanding, and it has taken a few centuries for Christian theology to recover from this. The real difficulty is that the biblical material remains far from clear to support such a view. Furthermore, we saw earlier that the Bible sees miracles as signs of God's activity. If God's work is "concealed" in chaotic systems, then is this really a sign?

In addition, such a view still has the danger of falling into the trap of seeing scientific law as prescriptive rather than descriptive. It is saying that in chaos the laws are less prescriptive. In the biblical sense, in miracles God is not overriding the order in the world. The scientific laws are regularities of the way God sustains the universe. The unusual phenomena which amaze us may be part of a deeper unity, rather like the Starship *Enterprise* in the satellite data program. Or they may be, from the human standpoint, deviations from what is regular, while for God they are changes to the regular ordering of natural events.

As with quantum theory, chaos does not at the moment give us an easy way to understand miracles, but I think that it does give us another way forward in understanding how God may interact with the physical world.

Uncivilized good sense, education, and learning

We have seen that one of the arguments against miracles, the Newtonian universe, does not hold in the face of modern science. But before we go on to thinking more about how God may work in the universe we need to respond to one of the other great arguments that dismissed miracles. This was the onslaught of David Hume on the evidence for God acting in the universe in unusual ways. Here science was used in a much more subtle way, pitting the evidence for miracles against the evidence collected in understanding the laws of nature. Might the passage of some three centuries since Hume and the development of science weaken this type of argument also? In particular, how might science look at the resurrection?

The first thing to be clear about is what we mean by the "laws of nature". As a physicist I know that our understanding of the laws of physics at the present time is not a complete and exhaustive description of the laws in themselves. The history of science readily illustrates this as scientific models change in the most unexpected of ways. Up until 1999, physicists believed that the universe would end either by slowing down in its expansion rate forever, or, if gravity was strong enough, the expansion would be reversed into a contraction and the universe would end in a Big Crunch. It was going to be one of these possibilities, and by measuring how much mass there was in the universe we would be able to tell between them. Then, an experiment designed to do just that showed a completely unexpected result. Observing distant supernovae explosions showed that the expansion rate of the universe was increasing – the universe was accelerating due to a large amount of dark energy, the origin of which still remains unknown.

History is littered with such changes in scientific models. The philosopher Thomas Kuhn (1922–96) called them "revolutions", although that image may push the reality of change too far. It is certainly better to see our current scientific models as giving us a tightening grasp of reality. Hume did not give sufficient attention to this understanding. Some scientists still have a naïve view of science which sees scientific models as literal and full representations of reality. However, a more coherent understanding is that of critical realism, which sees the provisionality of our description of the laws. These descriptions demonstrate an increasing verisimilitude – that is, as science progresses they are increasingly similar to the laws. However, our current scientific understanding should not be used as the basis to rule out the possibility of new phenomena or more exhaustive models. That is why all scientists place such emphasis on observational evidence, for ultimately that shapes our models.

This is a reminder of the folly of saying that our scientific understanding rules out miracles. Scientific laws are the regularities that we have discovered about the universe. All are subject to possible modification as more data becomes available, and if there are exceptions then we look for an explanation in terms of other laws. It may be that some phenomena appear miraculous not because they are breaking scientific laws but simply because they reflect a deeper, truer reality that our present understanding does not reach.

The second area of concern with Hume's view is in the way that he questions evidence. To write off eyewitness testimony because it comes from uncivilized people or because people may have a bias in recounting evidence would undermine a great deal of how we deal with evidence in modern society. Would courts revert to an earlier time when only educated men were able to give evidence? In a legal setting a person's testimony is assessed for consistency, honesty, first-hand experience, and other such criteria, rather than whether the witness has a PhD in astrophysics.

Then Hume questions evidence for rare events. To my

mind, as an astrophysicist, this has always been unconvincing. To say that we only believe things that have happened a large number of times – which on the surface seems to be a scientific statement – in fact would invalidate a lot of science. Of course science looks for regular patterns in the world, and so repeatability of an experiment is important. If one worker claims a particular result then others will try the same method to confirm the result. However, it is not always that simple. Some scientific events are unrepeatable – for example, the origin of the universe in the Big Bang. This is a one-off event and the way of studying it is more akin to history. Evidence is sought, which then enables us to construct our best model of what actually happened. One does not dismiss events simply because they are unusual or indeed unique. Whatever the event may be, the scientist will test the evidence and investigate further.

Finally, Hume would say that as he had never seen such an occurrence himself, this outweighs the testimony of others. But to say that we only accept things we experience ourselves is obviously untrue. How much do we actually experience ourselves? We are always accepting the testimony of others. Few of us bother to work through the formal proofs of mathematics, but we accept the arithmetic of our bank statements. We use what is generally accepted. Of course we weigh the testimony of others to an extent by our own experiences and the evidence they provide, but there are some events which we never can experience for ourselves. I do not have to spend the millions of pounds necessary to build a particle collider for myself before I accept the existence of the Higgs particle. Nor do I need to test a jet engine myself before I step inside an aeroplane for the first time.

Hume is too idealistic and pessimistic in how we actually assess evidence. He tends to talk in generalities rather than considering specific events. For many events there is going to be evidence for a particular interpretation and evidence against. What we do is to weigh up the evidence and take a decision. We never get proof in the big questions of science, but so what; that is not the way the world is.

Many people today rule out the possibility of miracles because of too simplistic a view of science or evidence. A better "scientific" approach would be to weigh seriously the evidence for or against particular miracles. This involves looking at different explanations of the same event and seeing which is more likely. Perhaps the crunch comes on the resurrection. It is interesting that this was the example that Hume used. We agree that our normal experience is that dead people do not rise to a state where they will never die again. Do we dismiss this miracle on this basis, or are we willing to change our view of the world on the basis of evidence? Other books have gone into such evidence in a great deal of detail. It is enough here simply to note that the kinds of questions that one would need to examine are:

a. What is the historical basis and reliability of the New Testament which records the events of the death and resurrection of Jesus?

Many people have dismissed the accounts as unreliable propaganda written many years after the event. Now of course, the Gospels were written for a purpose, and that purpose was not just to record historical fact but to present the good news of Jesus.

However, if we discounted all ancient documents on this basis then there would not be much history left! It does not have to be an "either/or" question. The Gospels have now withstood years of study and criticism and still their historical reliability can be vigorously defended. There are differences between the Gospel accounts concerning details of the resurrection, but far from questioning their reliability, the fact that they are different confirms it. If they were all exactly the same, I guess we would be worried.

Finally, as historical documents go of that period, the New Testament books were written down very early. Paul's first letter to the Corinthians was probably written no later than thirty years after the crucifixion. Thus, Paul, in writing about the resurrection, is able to say to his readers that many who Jesus appeared to are still alive (1 Corinthians 15).

b. What is the best explanation of the empty tomb?

Christians in Jerusalem who were preaching the resurrection would have been quickly silenced if the tomb was not empty! A curious fact is that there was never in Christian traditions any record of tomb veneration. Now these things seem to indicate an empty tomb, but the real question is, why was it empty?

There have been many alternative hypotheses. Some have suggested that in fact on the morning of the resurrection the women went to the wrong tomb! Others suggest that the Romans or Jews stole the body. But all of these explanations fall on the consideration that the easiest way to stop early Christianity (which both the Romans and Jews wanted to do) was actually to produce the body. Others have suggested that the disciples stole the body, but this surely cannot be right, for many of them died for their belief that Christ was raised.

Finally, there have been many who have suggested that Jesus did not die on the cross but only passed out. In the cool of the tomb he revived and convinced his disciples he had risen. Well, one could believe that, if you were prepared to accept that a man cruelly beaten, exhausted, crucified, and checked by Roman soldiers who were "experts" on death, could by himself struggle out under a weight of spices and bandages, role a heavy stone away, overpower the tomb guards, and then convince the disciples that not only was he alive but he was the undisputed conqueror of death! It seems somewhat unlikely, to say the least!

c. What is the best explanation for the claimed appearances of the risen Jesus?

The New Testament claims that the risen Jesus was seen over a period of six weeks, on at least eleven different occasions by at least 550 people, many of whom were still alive when Paul wrote to the Corinthians.

Is their evidence to be discounted as simply hallucinations, or did they really meet with Jesus?

d. What is the best explanation for the growth of the church?

All the evidence of the Gospels is that the disciples were frightened and confused after the death of Jesus. They did not expect the resurrection and even doubted the first reports of the empty tomb. What transformed them into the roaring lions that preached and died for the risen Jesus? And what about the testimony of millions of Christians over 2,000 years who, in their own experience, have encountered the reality and life of Jesus?

Now none of these things prove the resurrection. But taken together they give at the very least strong evidence for the Christian claim that Jesus was raised on the third day. That conclusion cannot be forced. I guess one could always maintain another explanation for all of the evidence. But is it as strong or as comprehensive in the face of the evidence?

On the basis of this evidence, the most reasonable conclusion is that, in the words of the theologian Wolfhart Pannenberg, the resurrection bursts our view of the world. Our view is often that death is the end and that there is no victory for self-giving love. The resurrection points to a deeper reality. It becomes the model, "the first fruits", of our own resurrection. There is a sense also in the New Testament that the resurrection is an outcome of a spiritual "law" that self-giving love cannot be held by death, "But God raised him from the dead ... because it was impossible for death to keep its hold on him" (Acts 2:24).

Now if the evidence for the resurrection is convincing we then have to accept that God can on occasions work in, through, and beyond the physical laws to do unusual things for specific purposes. This, it seems to me, is why Wiles works so hard in trying to explain the resurrection away as just a myth in his picture of a "sit back and watch" God.

A free God in an open universe

The picture I have been developing is that science does not rule out God responding to prayer in specific and unexpected ways. Yet there is a third issue with miracles – that of the problem of evil. In fact, it is a combination of Newtonian science and the problem of evil that has led to some of the models of God's activity described in the last chapter.

I was once a guest on a live BBC radio phone talking about science and faith. After talking about the possibility of miracles, the interviewer said, "Dr Wilkinson, we have 30 seconds before the news: could you tell us why God allows war, suffering, and death?" I did not have an easy answer then and I still do not have an easy answer. In fact, I do not even have a complex answer. I have struggled with this question throughout my Christian life, and as I detailed in Chapter 1, I struggle both intellectually and personally. Yet I am not prepared to allow the unanswered question of the problem of evil to control my whole view of how God acts in the universe, to the extent that theologians such as Wiles do. This is for two reasons. The first is that as a scientist I am used to assessing evidence for a model, which consists of supporting evidence but also has unanswered questions or sometimes evidence against. I come to a judgment about the weight of the evidence. For me, the evidence of the life, death, and resurrection of Jesus is so overwhelming in demonstrating the goodness and love of the God who is creator and at work in the universe now. Second, the God I see in Jesus is a God who shares the pain of evil. This is not an explanation of why such things happen, but it is a reassurance that in some way God cannot flick a switch and suddenly make everything better. This is enough for me to hold the unanswered question of the problem of evil.

However, I would not be a good scientist or indeed theologian if I did not continue to explore, give serious attention to, and struggle with the unanswered question. The problem of evil of course has been discussed in detail over many centuries by philosophers and theologians.[62] It has been used not just to argue that God cannot answer prayer but has also been used as an argument against the very existence of God. Various "defences" have been suggested to try to explain why a good God exists in the face of the reality of evil, such as the following: evil is due to God's granting of human free

---

62 Tooley, M. (2013). "The Problem of Evil". *The Stanford Encyclopedia of Philosophy*. Zalta, E. N. (ed.): http://plato.stanford.edu/archives/sum2013/entries/evil/

will; a world with evil in it is the best possible of all worlds; a world with evil provides an environment in which people, through their free choices, can undergo spiritual growth; and evil may ultimately be due to the immoral actions of supernatural beings.

While each of these insights may explain some experiences of evil they do not provide comprehensive answers to the problem of evil. For example, a world of "soul-making", as suggested by the philosopher John Hick, in which growth comes through experiences of both joy and pain, has some merit but does not come near to helping us understand experiences of excessive suffering.

Philosopher Alvin Plantinga comments:

> ... we cannot see why our world, with all its ills, would be better than others we think we can imagine, or what, in any detail, is God's reason for permitting a given specific and appalling evil. Not only can we not see this, we can't think of any very good possibilities. And here I must say that most attempts to explain why God permits evil – theodicies, as we may call them – strike me as tepid, shallow and ultimately frivolous.[63]

I agree with Plantinga on this. Attempts to explain why God permits evil never paint a comprehensive and theologically satisfying picture. However, if we are prepared to avoid trying to give a simple answer to the problem of evil, we can build a

---

63 Plantinga, A. (1985). "Self-Profile". *Alvin Plantinga*. Tomberlin, J. E. and van Inwagen, P. (eds). Dordrecht: D. Reidel, p. 35.

picture which takes Scripture seriously, takes science seriously, and takes the existence of evil seriously.

Such an attempt has been made within a school of theological thought that has come to be known as "open" or "openness" theology. It has had a number of ingredients. Within mainstream theology since the 1980s it has been fashionable to see God's creative love always accompanied by vulnerability.[64] This sees the incarnation and the self-giving of Jesus as central. God chose to give human beings freedom – freedom to reject him and indeed to nail him to the cross. In this theology of kenosis ("self-emptying"), God limits himself through the giving of freedom. But what if God chose to limit himself not just to the giving of freedom to human beings but gave to the universe a degree of freedom to explore its own potentiality? Thus, God creates through an evolutionary process that includes chance, in order to give human beings the possibility of development, with the consequence of the risk of suffering.[65]

This suggests, from theological concerns, that God allows the physical processes of the universe to proceed freely. God is omnipotent but limits his own power to give freedom. God is omniscient in knowing everything that can be known but there is a degree of genuine uncertainty about the future. To some Christians this sounds not just radical but heretical.

---

64 Vanstone, W. H. (1977). *Love's Endeavour, Love's Expense.* London: DLT; Moltmann, J. (1985). *God in Creation: An Ecological Doctrine of Creation.* San Franscisco: Harper and Row.

65 Ward, K. (1996). *God, Chance and Necessity.* Oxford: Oneworld Publications.

However, this picture has been built upon by a number of evangelical scholars who have argued that this is indeed how the Bible sees God's relationship with creation. This has provoked one of the major controversies of the past decade in evangelical circles. One of its main proponents, Clark Pinnock, was asked to leave the Evangelical Theological Society on this issue. He argues that traditional theism, championed by Calvinism's view of an all-controlling sovereignty, was developed primarily from Greek philosophy, is profoundly unbiblical, and the God we thus encounter is "manipulative, futureless, motionless, remote, isolated".

Largely unaware of modern scientific developments, Pinnock argues on biblical and theological grounds that God creates a world in which the future is not yet completely settled and takes seriously our response. In particular, he emphasizes those passages of Scripture in which God is shown as a free personal agent who acts in love, changes his mind, cooperates with his people, and responds to prayer.

This leads to some different understandings of classical theological terms, as Pinnock describes:

> God's unity will not be viewed as mathematical oneness but as a unity that includes diversity; God's steadfastness will not be seen as a deadening immutability but constancy of character that includes change; God's power will not be seen as raw omnipotence but as the sovereignty of love whose strength is revealed in weakness; and God's omniscience will

not be seen as know-it-all but as a wisdom which shapes the future in dialogue with creatures.[66]

Pinnock speaks of the "most moved mover" in contrast to the "unmoved mover" of classical theism. He argues that this understanding of the providence of God has significant practical consequences in the areas of prayer, lifestyle, friendship with God, freedom, and guidance.

This view builds on the insights of chaos to suggest a world that is open to the future and where God can genuinely respond to prayer. There are significant similarities here with process theology. However, openness theology would defend significant differences. First, its proponents argue that biblical authority is more important than the philosophical system, and second, there is a greater stress on God's transcendence. God is not dependent on the universe; he can intervene in acts of miracle and there will be a definite victory over evil at the end. In process theology God is limited to exercising only by persuasive power and that is in the nature of things rather than free will choice.

While pointing out a number of weaknesses, Gabriel Fackre nevertheless sees the strengths of the openness view as connecting with views of God's suffering love, taking seriously the biblical narrative, and giving reality to the experience of daily prayer.[67] I would agree with this. An open

---

66 Pinnock, C. H. (2001). *Most Moved Mover: A Theology of God's Openness*. Grand Rapids: Baker, p. 27.
67 Fackre, G. (2002). "Review", *Theology Today*, 59, pp. 319–323.

future gives the physical and theological space for God to work in answer to prayer.

Yet we must be careful not to go too far. Within Scripture, hope for the future is built on an understanding that God the redeemer is the same as God the creator (Isaiah 65:17–25). Whatever the circumstances, creation is not limited to its own inherent possibilities because the God of creation is still at work. Thus, the sovereignty of God in creation is the basis of hope that God will transform this creation into a new heaven and new earth. The key question for open theologies is whether this sense of God's overall sovereignty in bringing the story of creation to new creation is given strong enough emphasis. As the biblical scholar Richard Bauckham comments:

> *A God who is not the transcendent origin of all things but a way of speaking of the immanent creative possibilities of the universe itself cannot be the ground of ultimate hope for the future of creation. Where faith in God the Creator wanes, so inevitably does hope for the resurrection, let alone the new creation of all things.*[68]

The trouble often is that theologians go to one extreme or another – either the future is completely open or the future is entirely determined by God. Scripture is far messier! Pinnock emphasizes that open theology recognizes the primacy of Scripture. Yet, his presentation of Scripture is often selective. For example, he claims that the parable of the prodigal son

---

68 Bauckham, R. (1993). *The Theology of the Book of Revelation*. Cambridge: Cambridge University Press, p. 51.

(Luke 15:11–32) "dramatizes the truth of the open view of God".[69] This is fine as long as you do not complicate the matter by noticing that Luke joins this parable with two other parables that "dramatize" God as taking the initiative seeking a lost sheep and a lost coin (Luke 15:1–10). Here God's sovereignty in salvation is in dramatic tension with the gift of freedom. This neglect of emphasis on God's initiative also surfaces in Pinnock's description of a "bilateral covenant" in the Old Testament between God and his people. Yet the nature of the covenant depended on God's free act of grace and then Israel's response in the obligations of grace.

The openness view becomes more problematic when it comes to the long-term future. Its biblical emphasis wants to reflect the victory of good over evil but it is difficult to see how this might happen. Further, there is virtually no engagement with the major biblical themes of new heaven and new earth. Pinnock does use the analogy of God as the "master chess player". God is the consummate guide, allowing both freedom to the other person involved in the game and yet able to bring about ultimate victory. But does such an analogy represent genuine openness? The struggle to find an adequate picture shows the limits of the openness view in the light of God's ultimate purpose.

My theological roots are in the Wesleyan tradition. Because of this I want to reflect the importance of prevenient grace, which means that God's action is always first. Here is

---

69 Pinnock, C. H. (2001). *Most Moved Mover: A Theology of God's Openness*. Grand Rapids: Baker, p. 4.

Wesley's understanding of God's free and generous acting in the world, which both gives responsibility to his creatures and characterizes his own responsibility as creator and redeemer. In terms of personal salvation, God is active before conversion, during conversion, and in the growth to holiness. God is active in both preparing this path and in helping along the way. Therefore, in terms of models of providence, Wesleyan scholar Randy Maddox is right to comment (about process theology, but a similar point could be made about open theologies):

> *While the longstanding Wesleyan commitment to God's response-ability resonates strongly with the process emphasis on God's temporal, creative, and persuasive nature, it should be no surprise that this same commitment renders many Wesleyans less happy with the apparent restriction of God's role in the ongoing process of the whole of reality to only that of "lure". Is such a God still truly response-able? Where is the basis for eschatological hope within this restriction? Is there not a place for God to engage us more actively than this, without resorting to coercion?*[70]

This leads on to a further consideration. While an open future and a God who gives genuine freedom and responsibility to his creation means that our agency can make a significant difference, the goal of new creation gives our agency confidence. Advocates of openness see their position as a motivation to

---

70 Maddox, R. (2001). "Seeking a Response-able God: The Wesleyan Tradition and Process Theology?". In *Thy Nature and Thy Name is Love: Process and Wesleyan Theologies in Dialogue*. Stone, B. and Oord, T. (eds). Nashville: Kingswood Books, p. 142.

Christian responsibility and action, as our free human agency can make a difference. Gregory Boyd links genuine openness of the future to Christian responsibility: "Knowing that what transpires in the future is not a foregone conclusion but is significantly up to us to decide, we will be more inclined to assume responsibility for the future."[71]

While this is certainly the case, part of our motivation for Christian witness and action is not just the belief that we can make a difference, but also that the end is assured. Wesley's understanding of new creation gives confidence alongside opportunity. God's plan for new creation, demonstrated in the death and resurrection of Jesus, is about the eventual triumph of good over evil. We can believe that we can make a difference, but also that the end is assured. This gives confidence to Christians alongside opportunity, sustaining sacrificial action.

Difficult terrain, mistakes, and some insights

Just as the first explorers of the centre of the unmapped continent of Africa had to combat unfamiliar terrain, climate, and diseases, so our map of twentieth-century science and theological thinking may make us feel we would have been better to stay at home. The further trouble with exploring is that you do make mistakes. David Livingstone was one of the greatest explorers, who discovered numerous geographical features such as Victoria Falls and Lake Ngami. However, his great quest for the source of the Nile was never successful, and

---

71 Boyd, G. A. (2000). *God of the Possible: A Biblical Introduction to the Open View of God*. Grand Rapids: Baker, p. 94.

he mistakenly identified a source that was in fact the Congo River system.

In such an exciting and controversial area of theological thought, the tendency is always to try to get a simple and exhaustive answer, even if the terrain may be far from clear. We may need to tread more carefully. There are insights that this chapter has assembled that may need to be built into a bigger picture. It now is very clear that the Newtonian universe and Hume's critique of miracles does not provide the strength of argument that it once did. Indeed, the combination of twentieth-century physics and a more balanced view of the evidence for the resurrection makes us take seriously the possibility that God can respond to prayer in unusual ways beyond just changing the mind of the person who prays. This in itself is a huge step forward in theological thinking.

There then follow a number of possibilities. Consideration of God's vulnerability in the incarnation, the openness of quantum theory and chaotic systems, and the biblical material on God as a free agent certainly encourage the view that God can respond to prayer in distinct ways within the physical world. They also encourage the view that God has granted both human beings and the physical process of the universe real degrees of freedom. We must stress a limited amount of freedom; we as human beings do not have absolute freedom of choice. We are constrained by the nature of the world around us, physical and social, as well as being limited by our own abilities. This needs to be stressed also when raising the possibility of openness in the physical process. It is not the case that the whole of the future is unknown. Some of the future can be predicted and some of it is unknown.

If God has granted some freedom both to human beings and the physical process it would be difficult to understand if he did not reserve some freedom for his own action. The question is, then, how does God's freedom relate to his sustaining of the laws of the physics, his sovereignty in drawing this creation to new creation, and in respecting the freedom that he has granted?

CHAPTER 6

Lord, Teach Us to Pray

I heard a preacher once tell the following story about drought. It had not rained for weeks and the crops were slowly dying. The response of the churches was varied. Some simply accepted that it was all predestined and asked the Lord to show them clearly what they needed to learn. Some started to form a committee to look at what practical measures could be taken. Some decided to hold a meeting and pray for rain, although it was noticeable that only one woman brought her umbrella with her!

We began this book arguing that the key to prayer is how we understand God. It is not how we pray but who we pray to and how we think God can respond. It is the difference between taking an umbrella, having a sense that all is in God's hands, or putting together an action committee to help those in need. Yet it may be that it is not an either/or between these options. A big enough view of God may allow all of these options and others to be part of the life of Christian prayer.

The key to it all is whether God is the focus of prayer

or we are. It is easy to make our own concerns the centre of prayer. But D. L. Moody once said, "Spread out your petition before God, and then say, 'Thy will, not mine, be done.' The sweetest lesson I have learned in God's school is to let the Lord choose for me."

Indeed the supreme place where we are told how to pray begins not with practical instructions but with "who".

No need to babble in the presence of our Father

In the middle of the Sermon on the Mount, Matthew records Jesus' teaching on prayer. In chapter 6 of the Gospel, Jesus is talking about how some use prayer as a sign of their spirituality. His clear instruction is, don't do that! Don't babble in prayer with other people around. But surely Jesus is not saying to avoid prayer meetings? And surely there is something good about spending a long time in prayer? The answer to both is yes, but the point here is that good prayer expresses a concentration on God rather than it being used to impress others. Furthermore, be careful not to feel we can twist God's arm by endless babble. One image in the Old Testament immediately comes to mind at this point.

At Mount Carmel, the prophet Elijah challenges the prophets of Baal to a contest to show King Ahab the error of his ways (1 Kings 18:16–46). Two bulls are prepared on wood, and then prayers are said to Baal and then to the Lord for fire. The writer records:

*So they took the bull given them and prepared it. Then
they called on the name of Baal from morning till noon.
"Baal, answer us!" they shouted. But there was no
response; no one answered. And they danced around the
altar they had made. At noon Elijah began to taunt them.
"Shout louder!" he said. "Surely he is a god! Perhaps
he is deep in thought, or busy, or traveling. Maybe he is
sleeping and must be awakened." So they shouted louder
and slashed themselves with swords and spears, as was
their custom, until their blood flowed. Midday passed, and
they continued their frantic prophesying until the time for
the evening sacrifice. But there was no response, no one
answered, no one paid attention.*

In fact, part of Elijah's taunt could be translated, "Is your god
on the toilet?" The whole point is that it does not matter the
kind of prayer that is said if there is no God to answer it. By
contrast, Elijah's knowledge of and confidence in the Lord
leads him to a very different outcome:

*At the time of sacrifice, the prophet Elijah stepped forward
and prayed: "Lord, the God of Abraham, Isaac and Israel,
let it be known today that you are God in Israel and that
I am your servant and have done all these things at your
command. Answer me, Lord, answer me, so these people
will know that you, Lord, are God, and that you are turning
their hearts back again."*

*Then the fire of the Lord fell and burned up the sacrifice,
the wood, the stones and the soil, and also licked up the
water in the trench.*

When all the people saw this, they fell prostrate and cried, "The Lord – he is God! The Lord – he is God!"

The Lord's Prayer

In the Sermon on the Mount Jesus gives us a model of prayer which focuses first and foremost on who God is. The Lord's Prayer is incredibly simple and incredibly comprehensive. It has become such a formal part of public worship in many different traditions of the church. Indeed, I have experienced some churches where great anger is caused if the worship leader misses out the Lord's Prayer. But the model of prayer is not there to give us practical advice that must be followed by simply repeating the words at every time of prayer. It is a model of how we should understand God and his purposes in the world.

It is interesting that it begins with "our Father". It links the person who is praying to other believers. Prayer is not just about "me and my God". We have often individualized prayer by our Western obsession that the individual is at the centre of everything. Faith has become privatized. While the Gospels record instances where Jesus goes to pray alone, the Acts of the Apostles has numerous examples of people praying together. Following Pentecost, they "devoted themselves to the apostles' teaching and to fellowship, to the breaking of bread and to prayer" (Acts 2:42), and as we have seen met together regularly and especially in times of opposition or difficult decisions.

Part of the result of praying together was a renewed vision of the nature of God. In Acts 4:23–30, the group of believers, in the face of the first wave of threats and imprisonment of Peter and John, pray together, reminding each other of the power of God as creator which they experienced in Jesus. Luke notes, "After they prayed, the place where they were meeting was shaken. And they were all filled with the Holy Spirit and spoke the word of God boldly" (Acts 4:31). I have been moved in praying with others to a new vision of God. There is something very special in the prayer of other believers which lifts me into a new encounter with God. This can be in the prayers of those who have gone before us in the Christian faith expressed through liturgy or hymns. Indeed, I find the hymns of the Methodist revival in the words of the Wesley brothers to be especially helpful in both expressing my prayers and showing me more of God. But it is not just the gifted writers of songs and prayers that help me. I find heartfelt and honest prayers (however expressed) take me deeper into an experience of God. There is a theological foundation for why this communal or corporate aspect of prayer is so important. It expresses that to be human in the image of God is to be in community, just as God in the persons of the Trinity exists in a community of love.

Whether it be in a family or marriage setting, with friends before a meal, in the midst of church meetings (not just the beginning and end "nod to God"), or in a small group or in the church prayer meeting, it is important to pray with others.

As I write this I have just been speaking in North Carolina. My friend Paul arranged the engagements and a number of visits for me to say hello to various people. He and his wife are marvellous lay Christian people, and he is always pausing and saying, "let's have prayer together". He also holds out his hands and everyone has to link hands and join in – not something that an uptight British academic always feels comfortable with, especially in the public setting of a pancake house! But it symbolizes in a powerful way "our" Father.

Praying to our Father

The term "father" is now so well known in Christian spirituality that we no longer notice just how unusual a statement it is. It is not an obvious thing that the creator of the billions of stars in the billions of galaxies can be called "Father" by people like us. And this is not a term for a kind of universal fatherhood, where we call God "Father" because we are all part of the family of human beings. This is an intimate personal term. This is to address God directly as Father, just as Jesus himself does. He tells us we can do it too.

The image of God as Father has been at the core of Christian spirituality. Caution has rightly been expressed that it may not be the best model for everyone. I have met countless people whose experience of their own father has not been good. If your experience is one of violence, fear, abuse or neglect from an earthly father, then beginning a prayer with "our Father" can be both painful and debilitating. Here it is important that the Bible uses many more images of God than just a father – from a mother hen (Matthew 23:37) to a shepherd (Luke 15:3–7). It is also important to learn and work with the image of God being a good and perfect father. In fact, earlier in the Sermon on the Mount, Jesus has already referred to the perfection of his heavenly Father (Matthew 5:48). For some of us it takes time to understand this, and it is very easy to project the inadequacies of our parental experience onto God. This can affect how we pray a great deal.

The consistent reading of the Scriptures takes us back to encountering the nature of this perfect heavenly Father. In his book *Praying with Jesus*, Rob Warner notes what this means:

> *A father is meant to be someone you can trust. Someone you can turn to in moments of need. A good father wants to cultivate in his children a sense of confidence and security. He becomes a safety net for their self-belief, not a brooding and fearful shadow in the background, a cold-hearted and over-demanding disciplinarian.*[72]

I struggle with being a father, and my wife and kids would give all the evidence needed for such a statement. When our son was born, someone said to me the first eighteen years are the worst! Well it's been twenty years now and I am still having to work hard. The joys of course are massive. What I struggle with is not the late night chauffeuring; I struggle with how to respond well to requests for help without wanting to

---

72 Warner, R. (1999). *Praying with Jesus*, London: Hodder and Stoughton, p. 14.

take over situations where I see the danger of things going wrong – when to say "yes", when to say "no", and when to say to myself "keep out"! To nurture a relationship inevitably involves tensions that walk in between the indulgent, the dictatorial, and the uncaring. If there is some limited parallel between our experience in human relationships and God's relationship with human beings, then we might expect that in prayer God responds neither as indulgent parent, dictator, nor uncaring deity.

The Lord's Prayer goes on to stress immediately that this Father is "in heaven" and therefore there is a qualitative difference between God and us. We need to be careful here not to interpret this in the philosophy and imagery that we have inherited from Western culture, heavily influenced by Greek dualism. For the biblical writers heaven was not seen as a greyish shadowlands of immaterial spirits. Throughout Matthew's Gospel, the presence and the power of God in the coming of Jesus is referred to as the "kingdom of heaven" (Matthew 3:2) and it is used consistently to describe the difference between God and the things of this world (Matthew 7:11; 23:9). In this Matthew is saying that God's kingdom is unexpected and fundamentally different from the kingdoms of this world. As New Testament scholar Jonathan Pennington points out:

> *Matthew has intentionally taken the cosmological language of heaven and earth from the OT and has used it to communicate the urgently eschatological message of Jesus. A*

new day has dawned with the coming of the Kingdom. All is
overturned because of the epochal reality of the incarnation,
life, death, and resurrection of the Lord Jesus ... this way of
speaking provides the framework of a symbolic universe that
encourages the disciples to align themselves within the world
with a different vision and set of values.[73]

To recognize "our Father in heaven" is not only to remind ourselves of the infinite greatness and power of God, but it is also to align ourselves in prayer with a different set of values to those so prevalent in the world. Where the greed for power, fame, and fortune can often be the overriding motivation for life, prayer with this God at the centre takes our natural desires and changes them in the light of God's kingdom. Prayer becomes not just asking but learning. It fosters the process that Paul speaks about in Romans 12:2: "Do not conform to the pattern of this world, but be transformed by the renewing of your mind. Then you will be able to test and approve what God's will is – his good, pleasing and perfect will."

Indeed, the Lord's Prayer goes on with "hallowed be your name". Former Archbishop of Canterbury Rowan Williams helpfully points out that in the Old Testament the name of God points us to his presence, his beauty, and his power. To ask that God's name is hallowed is to ask the following:

... that in the world people will understand the presence
of God among them with awe and reverence, and will
not use the name or the idea of God as a kind of weapon

73 http://www.sbts.edu/resources/files/2010/02/sbjt_121_pennington.pdf

to put other people down, or as a sort of magic to make
themselves feel safe... So "Hallowed be thy name" means:
understand what you're talking about when you're talking
about God, this is serious, this is the most wonderful and
frightening reality that we could imagine, more wonderful
and frightening that [sic] we can imagine.[74]

Here, right at the start of Jesus' instruction on how to pray, is the importance of recognizing who God is. Sometimes it is so easy to forget this, as we get wrapped up in the practicalities of prayer or our own emotional concerns. It is also easy to be carried along in the Christian life and to stop thinking about these things – to recite the Lord's Prayer without ever engaging our brains, never mind our hearts.

Sometimes the experience of unanswered prayer is a moment when we come to a new understanding of who God is, as we struggle and reject some of the cultural images of God that we have uncritically accepted. It is tragic that some folk are so hurt in the experience of unanswered prayer that they reject God completely. It is a wise pastor or a friendly Christian who will need to listen to stories of unanswered prayer and help others to rediscover the biblical God. The Anglican evangelist David Watson, when encountering people who proclaimed that they did not believe in God, would say, "tell me about the god you don't believe in", and then he would often be able to say, "I don't believe in that kind of god either. Can I share with you the God that I believe in?"

---

74 http://www.bbc.co.uk/religion/religions/christianity/prayer/lordsprayer_1.shtml

But it is not only in the experience of unanswered prayer where we need to continually go back to examine the type of God we believe in. Earlier we noted Elijah's contest with the prophets of Baal. The Lord brings fire, answering Elijah's prayer, and Elijah is triumphant. Yet the writer of Kings continues the story, saying that Jezebel threatens immediately to kill Elijah (1 Kings 19:2). After such a demonstration of God's power in answered prayer one might expect Elijah would be unperturbed by such a threat. In fact, this great prophet is so spooked that he runs for his life, goes into the wilderness, and prays "that he might die" (1 Kings 19:4). With brutal honesty he complains to the Lord that he has had enough, and even though the Lord continues to provide for him he hides in a cave (1 Kings 19:4–9). In this state God meets with him:

> And the word of the Lord came to him: "What are you doing here, Elijah?"
>
> He replied, "I have been very zealous for the Lord God Almighty. The Israelites have rejected your covenant, torn down your altars, and put your prophets to death with the sword. I am the only one left, and now they are trying to kill me too."
>
> The Lord said, "Go out and stand on the mountain in the presence of the Lord, for the Lord is about to pass by."
>
> Then a great and powerful wind tore the mountains apart and shattered the rocks before the Lord, but the Lord was not in the wind. After the wind there was an earthquake, but the Lord was not in the earthquake. After the earthquake came a fire, but the Lord was not in the fire.

And after the fire came a gentle whisper. When Elijah heard it, he pulled his cloak over his face and went out and stood at the mouth of the cave.

1 Kings 19:9–13

Here God meets with Elijah and recommissions him. The experience may be extreme but it is not unfamiliar to Christian people over the centuries. I once listened to a preacher at a Christian convention speaking on this passage. He felt at such a convention he needed to be dramatic and involve the audience, but he got a little too carried away. He marched up and down the stage with the rhetorical device of saying, "Was God in the wind?" and then shouting, "No!" He used this for earthquake and fire, and then said, "And was God in the gentle whisper?", to which he shouted "No!" Confused as to where he was, he meekly said, "Well, I've forgotten where he was." In the "success" of answered prayer it is very easy to build a picture of God which is far from reality. Rather like superstition, if one form or formula of prayer seems to lead to a response from God that we want we repeat it or indeed offer it to other people as a guaranteed way of getting prayer answered. Such an approach denies the centrality of God, who works and speaks in many and various ways.

In the name of the Father, Son, and Holy Spirit

Why do so many Christian prayers conclude with the words, "in the name of the Father, the Son, and the Holy Spirit"? It is not a formula that is used within biblical prayers. There is something of it in Ephesians 5:20, where one of the marks of God's new community, the church, is to be "always giving thanks to God the Father for everything, in the name of our Lord Jesus Christ". It has a parallel in Colossians 3:17, "And whatever you do, whether in word or deed, do it all in the name of the Lord Jesus, giving thanks to God the Father through him."

It is explicit in the commission of the disciples by the resurrected Jesus at the end of Matthew's Gospel: "Therefore go and make disciples of all nations, baptizing them in the name of the Father and of the Son and of the Holy Spirit" (Matthew 28:19).

It is not surprising that such a formulation is not found explicitly in many places in the Bible. The Trinitarian understanding and liturgical practice of the church grew out of the experience of encountering God as Father, encountering God in Jesus, and encountering God as the Holy Spirit. It was not created as an easy theological answer or an elegant structure for understanding God. Indeed, Christian theologians continue to struggle with how to talk about the Trinity, as any preacher unfortunate to have to preach on Trinity Sunday will quickly tell you.

One of the characteristics of *Christian* prayer is that it is prayer that takes the Trinitarian nature of God seriously. This does not mean that every prayer has to invoke the name of Father, Son, and Holy Spirit, but the overall structure of Christian prayer should reflect this nature of God. A great deal of prayer for many people stays with "father". There are problems with this. As we have seen, an earthly image of father can become the template on which an understanding of God is drawn. Or it is easy to simply see the father as the supreme being of the philosophers. The tendency therefore is to go for an elegant philosophical solution of the "sit back and watch" God or the "working in the mind" God. Sometimes in philosophy we prefer the simple and fully consistent model. This can also be the case in Christian apologetics. In an attempt to show that the faith is reasonable, we produce models of God and how he works in the world that are simple to communicate and have an inner consistency which protects them from attack and criticism. Bishop David Jenkins was concerned to communicate God to those outside the church and Maurice Wiles was concerned to lessen the problem of evil. Even within individual Christian lives and thinking, as we try to make sense of our experience of the world and our experience of God, if we can find a model that is simple then that has great attraction.

But simple can quickly become simplistic. Remembering that God is Trinity forces us into a much more complex and dynamic view of God. God is both transcendent and immanent, acting as creator and sustainer, incarnate Christ who dies on the cross, and the power and presence of the Holy Spirit pervading the church and the world. This reminds us once again that the nature of God's action is complex and how we perceive it is also complex. The triune pattern is the way God relates to all things but it is also the means of understanding and expressing our knowledge of that relation. To the extent that we can understand how God is related to what goes on, we understand it "through Jesus Christ" and "in the Holy Spirit". Trinitarian thinking has often been neglected in the area of how God responds to prayer in favour of logic or science.

The Trinitarian God of the Bible is both creator and redeemer. That is not to say that God the Father is the creator and God the Son is the redeemer, for in the dynamic relationship of the Trinity all three persons are involved in both creation and redemption. For example, Paul can speak of Jesus in terms of the following: "For in him all things were created: things in heaven and on earth, visible and invisible, whether thrones or powers or rulers or authorities; all things were created through him and for him" (Colossians 1:16). And Paul can also write, "God was reconciling the world to himself in Christ, not counting people's sins against them" (2 Corinthians 5:19). But the Trinity is a constant reminder that the God of creation is also the God of redemption.

This makes a huge difference in thinking about how God answers prayer. Traditions within the Christian church have often separated creation and redemption. Some have stressed God's particular and unusual acts in history to the exclusion of his role in sustaining the whole creation. This has led to a definition of miracles as exclusively something over against the scientific laws.

Some time ago a man approached me asking for prayer for healing. I was happy to pray with him and lay hands on him. Then I asked him whether or not he had seen his doctor. He gave me a look that communicated that he was worried about my faith and said, "That's not very spiritual!" But to go to see a doctor is very spiritual! It is utilizing the wisdom that is built into the regularities of nature by the creator God. The skill of the doctor is made possible by being made in the image of God, and the human body's own powers of recovery once again are made possible by God.

It has to be "both/and" when it comes to God. We must stress the importance that the God of order upholds the universe with regularities. These regularities allow us to do science, to learn about the universe, to marvel at the wonders of creation, and they also allow us to grow in the moral sense. What moral sense might I develop if God overruled the consequences of bad actions or choices every time?

At the other extreme, some have so stressed creation that God has been given no freedom at all within that creation for particular acts. Miracles are defined exclusively as "the wonders of nature", such as the birth of a child. God is unable to do anything apart from sit back and watch. If God is moment by moment sustainer of the physical laws, then science could be seen as simply describing his normal mode of working. But God must be ultimately free to work in unusual ways.

If we see miracles in the context of a personal creator and redeemer God, we should expect both his sustaining and his particular actions. Indeed, we should expect a tension at times. The Bible reflects in this a tension of what we might call law and grace.

In an earlier book, I attempted to develop a personal analogy to try to express this tension. Imagine parents bringing up their child. If the child is to grow up responsibly then he or she needs to know various agreed norms or rules. If the parents are continually changing their minds, the child will find it difficult to grow in understanding or responsibility. However, it would be a poor childhood if there were not special treats, times when the normal rules were superseded by special acts of love. There will be times when bedtime is normally 9 p.m., but the highlights of the child's favourite football team are on the TV later and as a special treat the child can stay up. The development of the child requires a tension between law and what the Bible would call grace – that is, extravagant generosity.

Is such talk of tension and complexity really just a retreat to "it's all mysterious"? Sometimes that is just the way the world is. As a physicist I am well used to simplicity, complexity, and tension in the light of evidence. One of the amazing features of the physical world is that the laws of physics do have an elegance and simplicity to them that is both surprising and awe-inspiring. But sometimes that simplicity takes time to understand, and even with that simplicity complexity has to be held. The classic example is of course the dual particle and wave nature of light. There had been considerable debate over whether light was wave or particle from the Greeks through

Descartes and Newton. But mathematical and experimental work by Hooke, Huygens, and Fresnel, culminating in Thomas Young's (1773–1829) double slit experiment seemed to conclusively prove that it was a wave.[75] But then, in the twentieth century, the emission of electromagnetic radiation from a heated body, and Einstein's work on the photoelectric effect, where the energy of electrons liberated from a metal surface depends on the frequency rather than intensity of the light shining on it, indicated that light was made up of particles – photons. For some years, and still today in pre-university courses in physics, one simply has to accept that it is both/and rather than either/or because that is what the experimental evidence demands. It is only in the development of quantum theory and in particular quantum electrodynamics that we see why this is so. I therefore do not have any trouble as a theologian accepting concepts and models that may seem to be in tension with one another, as long as I have sufficient evidence on which to base this. I want to keep working on seeing whether there is a better model that might have a deeper understanding, but I am happy to accept complexity in the meantime.

Complexity has always been at the heart of Scripture, tradition, and experience concerning how God works in the world and answers prayers. In a chapter on "How God works in men's hearts", the great Reformed theologian John Calvin (1509–64) explores the complexity of how God, the

---

75 This experiment shines light through a plate which has two parallel slits in it to a screen beyond. The wave nature of light causes the light waves passing through the slits to interfere, producing bright and dark bands on the screen.

Chaldeans, and Satan are all active in the Chaldeans attack on Job's shepherds and flock (Job 1). Further, sometimes the biblical material claims that nothing happens that God does not make happen, such as in Isaiah 45:7: "I form the light and create darkness, I bring prosperity and create disaster; I, the Lord, do all these things." Yet sometimes it claims that time and chance have an important part to play, such as in Ecclesiastes 9:11–12:

I have seen something else under the sun:

The race is not to the swift
or the battle to the strong,
nor does food come to the wise
*   or wealth to the brilliant*
*   or favour to the learned;*
but time and chance happen to them all.

Moreover, no one knows when their hour will come:

As fish are caught in a cruel net,
*   or birds are taken in a snare,*
so people are trapped by evil times
*   that fall unexpectedly upon them.*

The biblical material is therefore very frustrating! Yet I cannot ignore it. I cannot selectively choose the parable of the prodigal son to argue that God, like the prodigal's father, simply sits and waits for human beings to change their mind. To do so ignores the parables of the lost sheep and lost coin which give an image of a God who takes the initiative and acts in the world. This difficult tension is a reminder that any one view of how God answers prayer might be neat and simple in the philosophy textbook but may be far too simplistic to do justice to a complex universe and the God who is beyond that universe. It is an easy trap to look for a simple philosophical or theological system and ignore some of the biblical data or indeed our experience of God's work in our lives.

Give us today our daily bread... but deliver us from evil

In a little book written in the 1960s, the North American theologian Albert Outler observes rightly that quantum theory does not allow us to construct a full model of how God works in the world, but cautions us as to the limits of science in predicting the future.[76] It is one of the few books of its era that tries to take quantum theory seriously. For Outler, God is undeniably in charge but also this world is a place where human freedom is real if limited. Grace is seen not only as the giving of freedom to what God has created but also God's active involvement in the world. Thus, because of grace, "he is truly free to allow evil as the dark shadow of corrupted good and yet sovereign to veto its final triumph".[77]

Outler is interesting in that he resists the tendency within certain theological thinking to attempt to produce a simple or logical philosophical picture. He sees God as both giving

76 Outler, A. (1968). *Who Trusts in God: Musings on the Meaning of Providence.* New York: Oxford University Press.
77 Outler, A. (1968). *Who Trusts in God: Musings on the Meaning of Providence.* New York: Oxford University Press, p. 96.

freedom and utilizing his own freedom in conquering evil. We saw that openness theology, in giving freedom to human beings and to the created order, then struggled to lay sufficient emphasis upon a God who, in the answering of prayer, is working to a big narrative of the triumph of good over evil.

This is a really important point for me. For a number of years I have been interested in the scientific predictions of the future. Many people think that science is all about optimism, transforming the future to be better and better. In fact, a recent book, *Hieroglyph,* is the result of a project between science fiction writers and scientists to imagine optimistic, technically grounded science fiction stories depicting futures achievable within the next fifty years. This, it is thought, would spur science itself to pursue such goals. But in part it was motivated by the dominance in current pop culture of a bleak and broken future, where science has caused all electricity to vanish (as in the TV series *Revolution*); the remnants of the human race to live in a broken-down space station (as in the TV series *The 100*); or human beings to be farmed as batteries by machines (as in the 1999 film *The Matrix*). Central to *Hieroglyph* is the belief that such pessimistic visions of the future limit people's abilities to dream big or think outside the box. One of the authors comments, "A good science fiction story can be very powerful. It can inspire hundreds, thousands, millions of people to rally around something that they want to do."[78]

---

78 http://www.bbc.co.uk/news/magazine-28974943

Yet despite hopefully inventing ways to locate missing odd socks and make fish and chips that contain no calories, the overall picture that science presents of the future is quite pessimistic. Science tells us not only that earth's environment is on a downward spiral, but an asteroid could also finish us off as well. Furthermore, the sun will eventually burn out and the universe itself is accelerating to its own "heat death", when all energy is dissipated in a murky soup. As we noted earlier, astronomers have discovered, quite unexpectedly, that the universe is accelerating in its rate of expansion due to some force, now called "dark energy". In this scenario, the universe becomes a cold and uninteresting place composed of dead stars and black holes, with the consequence that human life can no longer exist. It is interesting that in the same week that *Hieroglyph* appeared, Stephen Hawking raised the possibility that at very high energies the Higgs Boson[79] is so unstable that if we were ever to create such energies in a "planet size hadron collider" then it would destroy the whole universe. We would never even get to the cold dark heat death!

Now heat death is billions of years in the future, and producing a collision where the Higgs Boson becomes unstable is extremely unlikely. Nevertheless, such a view of the end of life as we know it inevitably colours our perception of life as it is now.

Thus, when it comes to the end of the universe, the cosmologist Paul Davies says that an "almost empty universe

---

79 This particle, whose existence was confirmed by experiments at the Large Hadron Collider at CERN, gives mass to particles in the universe.

growing steadily more cold and dark for all eternity is profoundly depressing" and Nobel Prize winner Steven Weinberg adds a final flourish: "The more the universe seems comprehensible, the more it also seems pointless."

In contrast, the biblical nature is full of hope. John Wesley saw new creation as the central image of hope in the New Testament. Wesleyan scholar Randy Maddox has helpfully characterized this "trajectory" in Wesley's theology as moving through new creation in the personal spiritual dimension, through the socio-political dimension, to the cosmic dimension.[80] The God of creation who shows his power over futility in the resurrection of Jesus is transforming this creation into a new creation. Towards this goal of transformation, God works in particular events and in long-term processes, hope being earthed in the evidence for the resurrection. Transformation of this creation is a key understanding in the biblical literature. This transformation is not just in physical matter or space-time but a transformation in context and relationships. Whatever freedom is given to this creation we cannot reach our potential in isolation.[81]

This vision of what God is doing is an encouragement to pray for the triumph of good over evil, whether it be in the physical universe or in human relationships. In this way prayer has to be said in the light of both creation and new

80 Maddox, R. L. (2002). "Nurturing the New Creation: Reflections on a Wesleyan Trajectory". *Eleventh Oxford Institute of Methodist Theological Studies*: Oxford.
81 Wilkinson, D. (2010), *Christian Eschatology and the Physical Universe*. London: T&T Clark.

creation. God is the one who responds to our prayers within the framework of sustaining the structures of this creation and his transformation of this world into new creation. We say both "give us this day our daily bread" and we say "deliver us from evil".

CHAPTER 7

Praying in the Light of What God Does

Ruth Etchells, with her characteristic ability to go to the heart of the issue, once wrote, "prayer has always been a bridge between the mundane and the holy". When I became Principal of St John's College in Durham University – a role which she knew so well – I would receive regular notes from her assuring me of her prayers for me and for the college. When we met for lunch, she was interested in the recruitment of students, whether the roof in a particular part of the college was leaking, how the boat club was doing, and whether the finances were healthy. Those things were as much a part of her prayer life as the spiritual health of those training as Anglican clergy.

Her books of prayers express the varied forms of her prayer life, where she speaks to God about doubt and failure, hope and joy, illness and healing. They remind me of the title of a book that she wrote many years before, *Unafraid to Be.* In it she makes a prophetic claim that there is nothing in her own academic subject of English Literature that could not be brought into the presence of God, even those pieces of literature and drama that fellow Christians dismiss as either offensive or trivial. It is her big vision of the God of creation and redemption, who reveals himself in the human flesh of Jesus Christ and is at work in both the world and the church, in the Holy Spirit, that gives her the confidence to believe that there is always a bridge between the mundane and the holy.

I have experienced that too in a small way. My own pilgrimage of prayer, as a disciple, scientist, and theologian, has brought me back time after time to the central question of how I believe God responds to prayer.

It is easy to be distracted about the form of prayer, or to slowly fall into a view of God that has little to do with the God of the Bible and in the long term corrupts the life of prayer rather than energizes it. I do not have any great secrets to share but I do have some cautionary words of which I constantly need to remind myself.

Don't make God too small

Albert Einstein wisely said, "Everything should be made as simple as possible, but not simpler." The bridge between the mundane and the holy is the wonderful gift that God gives to all, whether theologian, scientist, or small child. But understanding how it works in the sense of what God does is simply not that simple. The trouble of the legacy of Newton's clockwork universe is the imposition of a mechanical model upon not just the world but also the act of prayer. This is a long, long way away from the complexity of personal relationship between God and human beings that is demonstrated in the biblical material on prayer. As we have seen, even Newtonian mechanics itself is a far too simplistic view of the world. Chaos and quantum theory must be taken seriously. They may not provide easy gaps into which one can insert the intervention of God, but they do demolish the kind of universe which was thought to rule out the specific actions of God in the physical world. As Professor of Statistics David Bartholomew comments, "It is more important to establish that God could act in a world of chance than to discover how he does it."[82]

Equally, the models of God built up in Christian subcultures or indeed philosophical theology are inadequate in understanding that God may respond in lots of different ways in the world.

So, when we ask the question, "When I pray, what does God do?" there is a real sense that he is doing and can do a whole number of things. First, God is sustaining the structures and laws of the universe. Second, God is transforming this creation into new creation. Third, God transforms the person who prays to collaborate in building the kingdom. Fourth, God could be answering some prayers through working in the uncertainty and hidden arena of the quantum world and in chaotic systems. Fifth, God could work by transcending

82 Bartholomew, D. J. (1984). *God of Chance*. London: SCM Press, p. 143.

his normal ways of working for specific purposes. There is predictability and unpredictability, and a number of different avenues that God may choose to interact with the universe.

I think these are all possibilities that our current understanding of the world does not rule out. In Paris in the eighteenth century, there were reports of healings at the tomb of François de Pâris. This caused such a sensation that the cemetery was closed by royal decree in order to stop any public disorder. By the cemetery, a local wit put up a notice that read, "By order of the King, God is forbidden to perform miracles in this place". It may be too that our current understanding of the world is not exhaustive and thus there may be other models of God's action that we will need to be open to and consider carefully. While not retreating into hiding behind mystery, this does remind us that we need to be humble in trying to explain God's working or at least not rule possibilities out. The Anglican theologian Austin Farrer argued that we cannot conceive of God's way of acting in terms of our own, and therefore the causal joint between God's action and ours will always be hidden and lie beyond a full scientific description. For Farrer, each event in the universe will therefore have a double description – so-called "double agency". The event can be spoken of in terms of the providential action of God while at the same time have a full natural description in the laws of nature or the action of human agents. A similar approach has been taken by Sir John Houghton, a distinguished atmospheric physicist, who suggests that God is big enough to maintain consistency between God's particular answers to prayer while at the same time allowing for a complementary description in terms of natural processes.

All of this perhaps can be summed up in the title of J. B. Phillips' book, *Your God is Too Small* (1961). There are huge intellectual and theological challenges in all of this, but to reduce God in order to minimize these challenges is not the best option. Indeed, in the practice of prayer, whether in praise or in the struggle of intercession, there have been moments when I have encountered the greatness of God which is humbling, disturbing, and yet comforting. In those moments, I receive a new perspective on my life and my concerns – not easy answers but a different way of looking.

As I am a Christian in the Methodist tradition, you would expect me to keep coming back to John Wesley! But I do find his contribution as a theologian into this area very significant. The late Methodist leader and theologian Donald English commented, "Wesley's greatest contribution of all was his ability to face seemingly intractable problems and to place them into a creative tension which was not resolved but was life-giving."[83]

Thus he placed a Protestant understanding of salvation alongside a Catholic doctrine of perfection in a way that brought the experience of forgiveness and the desire for holiness together. In the area of prayer, I would want to try to do a similar thing. I want to resist any attempt to oversimplify

---

83 English, D. (1979). *From Wesley's Chair*. London: Epworth, p. 91.

the doctrine for the sake of resolving all tensions. Complexity and mystery must be maintained, especially if this is life giving.

In all of the theological discussion and alternative models, it is easy to forget that God at work in the world gives Christian lifestyle its "buoyancy and gracefulness".[84] To perceive God's gracious presence and activity is to respond in worship, see this life as good, and to be freed from ultimate anxieties so that we can live intensively in the present and hopefully towards the future.

Don't dismiss laser beams

While Bishop David Jenkins strongly resisted any sense of a laser beam God, John Polkinghorne has used the concept of a laser as a helpful model to talk about prayer. A laser is a device that emits light through a process of optical amplification based on the stimulated emission of electromagnetic radiation. The key way that a laser differs from other sources of light is because it emits light coherently. This allows a whole range of applications that are part of the everyday world. Lasers can be focused to a very small place, leading to the ability to cut patterns inside glass blocks. They produce a narrow beam over very long distances, which means that we can fire a laser at retro reflectors left on the moon by the Apollo missions, and then, by measuring the time for the reflected light to return, we can measure the distance to the moon (and indeed debunk all those conspiracy theories which say that the lunar landings

84 Outler, A. (1968). *Who Trusts in God: Musings on the Meaning of Providence.* New York: Oxford University Press, p. 123.

were all done on a Hollywood film set). This is possible because the mechanism of a laser puts all the oscillations of the light in phase. This is what gives a laser its enormous power.

Polkinghorne uses this as a model for prayer, seeing the "tuning of divine and human wills to mutual resonance through the collaboration of prayer".[85] I find this a helpful model in many respects. A laser shows that mutual resonance is able to achieve remarkable things. The bridge between the mundane and the holy is therefore a subtle interaction of our freedom and God's freedom (and indeed the proponents of open and process theology would add the degree of freedom given to the world). This interaction does change us, but it can also truly change the world. Thus, Polkinghorne writes, "he wishes our desire to be exercised in prayer that we may be able to receive what he is preparing to give. In other words, prayer is neither the manipulation of God nor just the illumination of our perception, but it is the alignment of our wills with his, the correlation of human desire and divine purpose."[86]

In this the exercise of our freedom and indeed any openness in the process of the world is constrained by this interaction. Does this somehow minimize the sovereignty of God or diminish his grace? Any constraint on God's power is his gift in love of freedom and the gift of prayer. It is a remarkable testimony to God's love that he involves our prayer, with all its weakness, selfishness, and insularity into the working out of his good purpose.

85 Polkinghorne, J. C. (1989). *Science and Providence*. London: SPCK, p.71.
86 Polkinghorne, J. C. (1989). *Science and Providence*. London: SPCK, p.70.

This gives me confidence to come to God as I am and be honest in prayer. I am going to ask for things that are selfish and indeed in the light of bigger concerns downright embarrassing. But the invitation from God is to come into a transforming conversation with him. As a parent there is delight in a conversation with my child even if it is a request for a pony, a car, or an ice cream! I would much rather have the conversation than no conversation at all.

Yet such an understanding of this personal relationship of prayer has to accept "your will be done". The mundane can be shaped by the holy and indeed can become holy as we allow our will to be in line with God's. Sometimes God's ways and God's responses to prayer will be completely unexpected. At the centre of the Christian story is a God who is both creator of the universe and the one who dies on a cross. This death of Jesus is the result of God allowing all the physical and biological processes that lead to death in the act of crucifixion to proceed in their usual way. Jesus had asked whether this cup of suffering could be avoided and I speculate that his disciples and family were also praying that this would not happen. Yet through the vulnerability of Jesus in the face of death God's work of salvation is done.

As we have seen, a number of contemporary pictures of God give the impression that the miraculous is always "on tap" to be claimed by faith. God has his own will, which is often at the time very difficult to understand. It may be that in the context of his sovereign will God does not produce the answers that we expect. Our role is to pray and ask his will to be done.

An insurance company once wrote to clergy publicizing new policies. As part of the policy was the claim to insure churches against acts of God! In prayer we need to be open to the will of God, looking to be transformed by the act of prayer and how God responds.

Don't try to explain away the difficult questions

Honesty is crucial in prayer, both with God and with one another. The Bible is of course a book with a purpose; it is not neutral in its stance. As John says towards the end of his Gospel, he has selected only certain things to pass on and "these are written that you may believe that Jesus is the Messiah, the Son of God, and that by believing you may have life in his name" (John 20:31). It is therefore remarkable that the writers of the Bible record stories of failure as well as success.

For example, when Paul goes to preach in the Areopagus in Athens, Luke records that some sneered, some invited him back, but overall he makes very few converts compared with some of the other places he visited (Acts 17:16–34). What has interested me is the way that some Christian preachers and commentators have reacted to this. Some have tried to give a reason, saying that Paul made a mistake in not preaching about the cross of Jesus and by becoming too philosophical with his audience. They link this with the fact that Luke says that after Athens Paul goes to Corinth, and Paul himself records that there he preached nothing but "Jesus Christ and him crucified" (1 Corinthians 2:2). Others have suggested that while there were not many converts, the converts he did make were very significant. But I think Luke is simply leaving us with the message that in some places Paul was not as successful as others, and he does not explain why.

Our tendency in prayer is sometimes just like that of some of the commentators on Acts 17, especially when we come to unanswered prayer. We either want to give a reason to explain it or we want to spin the story so that God does not look too bad! So we do not get answered prayer because we did not pray with enough faith or we prayed in the wrong way. Or we try to say that God answered our prayer in a different way. For example, we spent so much money in buying 10,000 Bibles to give to folk in our community and we prayed about it but only one Bible was taken – but it was always God's will for that one person to have a Bible! Of course, God does answer prayer in different ways and sometimes we do pray for the wrong things. But sometimes we just have to be honest and say prayers have not been answered, we have experienced failure not success, and we do not understand God's will in this matter.

As we saw in an earlier chapter, there are many instances of unanswered prayer in the Bible. They are told openly, without explanation and without embarrassment. To build a healthy prayer culture within churches, it is absolutely essential to tell stories of God's actions but not to publicly hide away from difficult experiences or questions.

If healthy prayer in groups is based on honesty, then honesty is also the key to health in our individual prayer life. The psalms are full of such honesty, such as complaining to God:

> *How long, Lord? Will you forget me forever?*
> *How long will you hide your face from me?*
> *How long must I wrestle with my thoughts*
> *and day after day have sorrow in my heart?*
> *How long will my enemy triumph over me?*
>
> (Psalm 13:2)

Then there are the downright embarrassing and at times horrific psalms:

> *Daughter Babylon, doomed to destruction,*
> *   happy is the one who repays you*
> *   according to what you have done to us.*
> *   Happy is the one who seizes your infants*
> *   and dashes them against the rocks.*
>
> (Psalm 137:8–9)

This is one of a series of so-called imprecatory psalms of calling down God's judgment on our enemies, which is so far away from Jesus' command to love. Now I can understand anger borne out of personal suffering, concern for God's name, and the triumph of the wicked. But these psalms allow this anger to come in the presence of God. Prayer can lack this authenticity. It is as if we are in the presence of someone with whom we have to use our posh voice and be on our best behaviour.

ʙut it is the people with whom we are most secure who can hear our anger and allow us to unburden ourselves so that it does not eat away at us as under-the-surface bitterness. There have been many moments in my life when I have shouted and complained loudly at God. I have felt disappointed; I don't understand what is going on and God seems to be a long way away. It is only when we are real with God about how we feel that he can transform us. The constant thread throughout the psalms is the goodness and power of God and how we can trust in him. It is only when we get this anger out that we can start to see that.

Don't think too small

Of all of the prayers in the New Testament, my favourite is probably the insight that is given into the prayer life of the apostle Paul in the letter to the Philippians:

> I thank my God every time I remember you. In all my prayers for all of you, I always pray with joy because of your partnership in the gospel from the first day until now, being confident of this, that he who began a good work in you will carry it on to completion until the day of Christ Jesus.
>
> It is right for me to feel this way about all of you, since I have you in my heart and, whether I am in chains or defending and confirming the gospel, all of you share in God's grace with me. God can testify how I long for all of you with the affection of Christ Jesus.
>
> And this is my prayer: that your love may abound more and more in knowledge and depth of insight, so that

*you may be able to discern what is best and may be pure
and blameless for the day of Christ, filled with the fruit of
righteousness that comes through Jesus Christ – to the glory
and praise of God.*

Philippians 1:3–11

Here Paul's prayer is infused with his knowledge of who God is and God's great purpose for the world. His prayer *flows from gratitude and is filled with joy* (verse 3), because he recognizes the gift of other people as partners in the gospel (verse 5). They are not just fellow workers but a new community and new family who share in God's grace (verse 7). Paul has been changed by this grace; he sees it in other people and so wants to affirm it. This leads to his prayer being based *on confidence in God's actions and intentions.* Confidence is such a key thing in how we grow and how we live. I don't mean overconfidence that leads to arrogance and carelessness, but a sense of security and a conviction that there will be victory. In sport confidence is such an important factor. A football team without confidence plays it safe, avoiding risks but at the same time is more prone to errors. However, a team with confidence can express itself more fully and has the energy to pursue the match deep into injury time at the end, believing that a win is possible. It is easy to lose confidence in prayer. This was certainly a temptation for Paul. Paul was physically absent from the church in Philippi, imprisoned and not in control while there were divisions in the church and attacks from outside the church. It would be easy to start to despair that this group of Christians that he loved so much would be buffeted off course. But his confidence was not in himself but in God's action and purpose, "being confident of this, that he who began a good work in you will carry it on to completion until the day of Christ Jesus" (verse 6). Paul is convinced that God is active, God is committed, and God is victorious because he has seen him at work in Jesus. In chapter 2 he will articulate that in a great hymn about the life, death, resurrection, and exaltation of Jesus (Philippians 2:6–11).

However, what really challenges me in this prayer is how his knowledge of his Lord leads to such big prayers (verses 9–11). If I am honest my prayer life by comparison is so trivial. I learnt as a child to say "God bless Daddy, God bless Mummy, God bless Auntie Hilda and look after me. Amen." Apart from changing the names sometimes my adult prayers are not too different! Here Paul prays that love may overflow more and more with knowledge and full insight. He longs that they discern what is best, be pure and blameless, and be filled with the fruit of righteousness. He does not want his brothers and sisters in Philippi to simply get through; he prays for excellence in their lives as Christians. It is a wonderful truth of the gospel that God through Jesus accepts me as I am, but that is only half the story. His purpose is to transform us into the holiness of Jesus and indeed to transform all things into a new heaven and a new earth.

Perhaps I do not pray enough because I do not have this big enough vision. It is a vision of who God is, not a vision of how faithful or creative I am in prayer. As Bishop Festo Kivengere once said, "I'm just an ordinary Christian. There are no extraordinary Christians anywhere, just ordinary ones saved by an extraordinary Saviour."

I was once a guest of the master of a college in a British university. Over Sunday morning breakfast he was telling me of some of the historic books that were in the college library. I had to go and preach but I wondered if I had time to see the books. What I thought would be a simple request involved quite a lot of arrangements. I assumed that the master would simply take me to the library and show me the books. In fact, the master had to get the college librarian out of bed, various doors had to be unlocked, and the books brought out of special storage. I became more and more embarrassed at causing all of this trouble early on a Sunday morning. I apologized profusely for asking for this. He replied with a smile, "Don't worry, you are talking to the master. I would have said no if it wasn't possible." I found in this a small picture of prayer. At its heart is a relationship which gives me confidence to ask, and the confidence that sometimes the answer will be no.

Our Master, Lord, and Saviour Jesus encourages us to pray, bridging the mundane and the holy. We find ourselves praying in a world of both law and grace, praying in a world between creation and new creation, praying in a world with mystery and signs, and praying in a world where God works and waits. "When I pray, what does God do?" is not an easy question, but it is one that I have found in my own life leads me deeper into knowing God and an excitement with the experience of prayer.